Praises, Promises, and Provisions

Lessons Learned from the Pen of the Psalmist

Kathy O'Brien

WESTBOW
PRESS®
A DIVISION OF THOMAS NELSON
& ZONDERVAN

WestBow Press books may be ordered through booksellers or by contacting:

WestBow Press
A Division of Thomas Nelson & Zondervan
1663 Liberty Drive
Bloomington, IN 47403
www.westbowpress.com
844-714-3454

Scripture taken from the New King James Version® Copyright © 1982 by Thomas Nelson. Used by permission. All rights reserved.

ISBN: 978-1-6642-6396-3 (sc)
ISBN: 978-1-6642-6398-7 (hc)
ISBN: 978-1-6642-6397-0 (e)

Library of Congress Control Number: 2022907215

Print information available on the last page.

WestBow Press rev. date: 5/18/2022

Contents

Introduction

The Challenge was on!

"Hey, teacher! Do you want to do a Bible challenge with me?" said one of my eleven-year-old students, with a smile on his face. He was shifting his body from one foot to another, anxiously awaiting my answer. I could not help but chuckle a little. Usually it was I who was presenting the challenges to my students. It did this teacher's heart good to see the roles reversed for a change.

"Hmm," I replied as I gave him a quizzical glance, "what do you have in mind?"

"Well, I really want to read through the entire book of Psalms. Do you know that it has the most chapters of any book in the Bible? I was wondering if you would like to do it with me. You could make sure that I read it from the beginning to the end, all one hundred and fifty chapters."

While I was delighted at seeing his enthusiasm to read a portion of the Bible, as his teacher, I was just a little curious as to what led this young student to want to read the entire book of Psalms. He normally was not a keen reader at all. In fact, I had noticed the struggle he often had just to find his way around the various pages of his Bible. I clearly saw a teaching moment standing right here in front of me.

"You know what? I would love to accept your challenge!" Instantly I saw a smile break out on his face that rocked my heart as a teacher. "But, if it is okay with you, I would like to add something extra to your challenge to help make reading God's Word a little more exciting for both of us."

"Okay!" he said. His feet were practically dancing as his level of excitement went up a few notches. "What? What do you want to add?"

"Do you know what a scavenger hunt is?" I asked.

"Oh, yes, I love doing scavenger hunts!" His excitement level went up a few more notches. "With scavenger hunts you have a list of objects to find, and if you find them all, then you win the hunt and you get a prize."

I gave a thumbs-up to his explanation. And before I could say anything, he quickly piped in.

"But I don't know how to play a scavenger hunt using the Bible. I've never done that before."

"Well, while we are reading each chapter, I would like for us to be watching for three things: praises, promises, and provisions."

"Oh, so we are looking for those three words. I can do that," he said, giving me another thumbs-up.

"Yes, we can look for those words and see if they are in our chapter readings. But we can also pay attention to the concepts of praises, promises, and provisions. What I mean by that is this: Does the psalmist praise God in any way? What is he praising God for? Is there a promise from God shared in the psalm? Is it a promise that we can claim too? Does God provide something for the psalmist? Does God provide food, shelter, help, strength, wisdom, or any other thing for the psalmist? We could scavenge our way through the book of Psalms, looking for those three things. I am almost certain if we play a little game of Bible scavenger hunt as we are reading, it will help us understand better what we are reading."

His reply came with dancing feet, a thumbs-up, twinkling eyes, and a smile that stretched from ear to ear. "You accepted my challenge, teacher. Now I will accept yours!" A high-five exchange sealed the deal between teacher and student.

The challenge was on!

Both of us agreed to keep a journal of all the things we found as we played this game of Bible scavenger hunt. Quite often we shared with one another the delight of discovered treasures.

"Who knew!" my student said one day. "Who knew that the book of Psalms had so many praises, promises, and provisions."

Who knew, indeed!

That teaching moment changed my student. He was surprised with the fun he had in reading God's Word, the Bible. He talked, with great excitement, about all the different things he learned. He discovered many precious treasures as he read through the book of Psalms. In accepting my part of the challenge, he was able to turn his dislike of reading into a game. It was a game that captured his attention—a game through which he learned to love God and His Word. God captured his young heart!

His was not the only heart touched. This teacher was also changed by her student's challenge. I loved his enthusiasm of doing something together with his teacher. I was thrilled that he wanted to overcome his difficulty with reading. I adored his reaction to God's Word and loved listening to him tell of the things he was learning as he read. Over the years, since this story happened, I have prayed for this young man—prayed that God would always be able to captivate his heart and life for His glory.

I have read through the book of Psalms many times in my life as a Christian. But this time, through this challenge, and through the Bible scavenger hunt of looking for the praises, promises, and provisions, my eyes were opened to things I had never seen before. My ears were listening to every word as I read the scripture out loud. My soul was opened to praising my God even more. My understanding found promises that had been claimed by the psalmist, that I could also claim as mine. My heart grew in gratitude as I realized that those things which God had provided for the psalmist, He would also provide for me. My hands clapped with excitement and my feet danced with joy at the precious treasures I had uncovered in the pages of the book of Psalms.

In the following pages of this book, I would like to share with you some of the praises, promises and provisions that we find as treasures in the book of Psalms. May your heart be blessed as you read my stories and share in the lessons learned.

Who knew? Who knew that the book of Psalms holds so many praises, promises, and provisions!

You will not know until you begin to read.

Our God Is Awesome

Let all the earth, fear the Lord; let all the
inhabitants of the world stand in awe of Him.
—Psalm 33:8

It was a few years ago that I had the privilege of meeting the most precious, never-to-be forgotten little six-year-old girl. She was beautiful inside and out. She had big brown eyes, brown hair tied up in pigtails, a smile that was missing its front teeth, and a personality that just made me laugh.

She made sure that I noticed her new pink dress and white shoes that she was wearing. Yet what I remember most was her conversation. She loved to talk with anyone who would listen. I loved talking to her because she had some very good things to say. Have you ever had a conversation with a six-year-old kid about God? Now that is one priceless conversation, let me tell you!

She did her best to describe God to me. "God is smart, probably the smartest person in all the world. He's probably old—older than my daddy, and of course older than my papa! My papa says God is older than dirt. Do you believe that? And God smiles like me. I know because He gave me my smile, and see"—yep, I saw that toothless smile!—"see what it looks like. And I think God might laugh too, but not as good as me. I work hard to keep my laugh funny. My papa likes my laugh, so I think God does too. But do you wanna know what I like best about God?"

With this she stood up and spread her arms out as wide as they could go, her eyes got big and glistened in the sunlight, and she rather loudly and boldly proclaimed, "God is wha-some! He really, really, really, really, really is wha-some! I tell you, He is wha-some!"

Bless her little heart, she could not say the word "awesome"; it just came out as "wha-some." I love that word! It is just so priceless!

I could not help but smile at her. I joined in on her jubilant praise party. "Yes, my dear little friend, our God is wha-some!"

Now every time I am outside hiking, picnicking, gardening, or simply taking the time to sit and enjoy God's beautiful creation around me, I think of that little girl. And I smile. She is almost all grown up now, but I am pleased to say that she still thinks her God is wha-some!

God is definitely wha-somely awesome! And He is worthy of all our praise!

The psalmist David loved to sing out the praise of God's awesomeness as well. Many of his psalms reflect his own attitude of worship and praise to an awesome God. One such psalm is psalm 66, which says, "Make a joyful shout to God all the earth! Sing out the honor of His name; Make His praise glorious. Say to God 'How awesome are Your works! ... All the earth shall worship You and sing praises to You; They shall sing praises to You; They shall sing praise to Your name' ... Oh, bless our God, you peoples! And make the voice of His praise to be heard" (Psalm 66:1–4, 6).

So what about you? When was the last time you thought about your awesome God? When was the last time you stood in awe of His creation around you? When was the last time you burst forth in jubilant praise to your awesome God?

Ah, go on, try it!

With the joyful enthusiasm of a six-year-old kid, not caring what anyone else thinks, start your own praise party for God.

Why not shout it loudly and boldly proclaim, "God is wha-some! He really, really, really, really, really is wha-some! I tell you, He is wha-some!"

It is guaranteed to make God smile!

I Choose to Praise God

Praise the Lord! Praise God in His sanctuary;
Praise Him in His mighty firmament! Praise Him
for His mighty acts; Praise Him according to
His excellent greatness! ... Let everything that
has breath, praise the Lord. Praise the Lord!
—Psalm 150:1-2

The psalmist David is one of my many favorite Bible characters. I love to study his life and times, learning all I can and hopefully taking to heart some of the lessons that his life teaches.

David was known as "a man after God's own heart" (1 Samuel 13:14), and his relationship with God is something to admire and seek to imitate. While his life was far from perfect (which is why I can relate to him!) and his relationship with God was not perfect either (so glad that God does not require perfection of us!), David set his heart on one thing, and that was to seek after his God with all his heart. I love that. That is the kind of life example that I desire to follow.

There is something, though, that really impresses me about David. It stands out to me every time I read about David or hear a sermon about him. Throughout his lifetime, David had a heart that was not afraid to burst forth in bold praise to his great God. David chose to praise God.

It did not matter whether David was tending his father's sheep in the field, relaxing at home with his family, facing the giant that no one else wanted to fight, singing before King Saul, running for his life from someone who wanted to kill him, fighting the enemy on the battlefield, encouraging his soldiers as they returned tired from war, feasting at the fully loaded banqueting table, or pursing his kingly duties from the regal palace. One would often find David offering up his praise to God. David chose to praise God.

The book of Psalms is full of David's songs of praise to his mighty God. Psalm 150 is just one example. It is one reminder of a heart full of praise to a worthy and holy God.

There are so many ways to praise God: quietly in our hearts, loudly with our voices lifted high, on any instrument of choice, in a solitary place, or in a crowd. We can praise God.

There are many reasons to praise God: for who He is, for what He has done, for victories won, for good news received, for answers to prayer, for His creation round about us, or for any reason at all. We can praise God.

There are various places where we can burst forth in praise: in the sanctuary, in our homes, in our workplaces, out in the middle of God's creation, in a hospital bed, in a jail cell, or in any place we go. We can praise God.

Yet this is the part of David's example of praise that gets me. David *chose* to praise God. Praise, for David, was an intentional choice! It did not matter whom he was with; he chose to praise God. In good times, bad times, joyful or sad times, and times of peace or war, David chose to praise God.

I must choose to praise God too!

Praise comes easy when things are going great. Well, for me it does. Praise is good when God blesses me with abundant things. Praise is an outstanding way to thank God for His answers to prayer. Praise is great when I gather with fellow believers and, together in one spirit, we lift up our praise to God in worship of Him. But what about when things are not so good?

I must choose to praise God! In every situation of life, I choose whether to praise or not.

- I choose to praise God when I am having a really bad day and everything seems to be going wrong and I really want to run away from it all. I choose to praise God at these times because I know that wherever I am, there God will be as well to bring comfort to my troubled heart.
- I choose to praise God when relationships are filled with misunderstandings, false judgments, lies, gossip, jealousy, and strife. I choose to praise God at these times because I know that God will speak peace into those relationships and will do His perfect work within His perfect time to bring about healing, calm, and restoration.
- I choose to praise God when the financial month has ended long before the calendar month and there is still a stack of bills waiting to be paid. I choose to praise God at that time because I know Jehovah Jireh is my provider, and I trust Him to meet those financial needs.
- I choose to praise God when the doctor says I need surgery and I say, "What, now?" I choose to praise at these times because He is the perfect healer, and He will guide the surgeon's hand in fixing what does not work right.
- I choose to praise God when so many friends are being taken away from this world by the dreaded enemies of cancer, COVID-19, and other serious illnesses. I choose to praise God at these times because I know those precious friends are now in

the presence of their God, completely healed of all their diseases.

- I choose to praise God when … My list could go on and on!

But do you see what I am saying? Praising God is our daily choice. It is a moment-by-moment, all-throughout-the-day kind of choice.

Praise should never be influenced by those around us. It should be instrumentally instructed by the contents of our hearts. Praise should never be dependent on our current circumstances being good or right or even fair. Praise is not based on our feelings at a certain moment of time. We can feel perfectly lousy and still choose to open our hearts, lift up our voices, and burst forth with praise to the God who loves and cares about us.

Praising God is a choice. It is our privilege. It is our way of acknowledging that our great God is present with us (never to leave us or forsake us!). He is there, right in the midst of our circumstances. Praising God is a means of giving thanks for all the great things God has done for us, has given to us, and has answered on our behalf. Praising God is boldly declaring His faithfulness, His greatness, His power, and His majesty to the world around us. It is an honor to lift up our hearts, our voices, our hands, and our very beings in praise and worship to a God whose heart we seek after.

"Let everything that has breath, praise the Lord!" (Psalm 150:6).

I choose to praise God today!

Praise the Lord!

From the rising of the sun to its going down,
the name of the Lord is to be praised.
—Psalm 113:3

Our little dog, Max, and I were all set for our evening walk together. It was still hot and muggy from the long monsoon summer day. In all probability, our Maltese / shih tzu mix of a dog would not go very far at all, and yet I figured that the walk would do us both a little good.

I just wish it would rain and bring us a little relief from this heat, I thought as Max and I walked down the driveway and started out for a good night's walk. Then it happened.

I looked up into the sky ahead as the sun was setting for the evening. I was stunned at the beauty my eyes were beholding.

I could see a quarter of the golden sun dipping down behind the mountain range. Extending from the center were golden-yellow rays lying atop the horizon. The remaining clouds took on the colorful hues of orange, red, pink, and purple, while patches of blue sky lingered. The trees darkened as the colors of the sunset lit up the sky. It was a magnificent picture that brought peace and calm to the end of a busy day.

I stood there with Max at my side, staring breathlessly

at the beautiful sight before me. I took in its awesomeness. "Wow, God, this is amazing!" I said out loud. God's handiwork is always amazing! But that night it was spectacular!

In that instant, God brought the verse of Psalm 113:3 to my mind. I said it a couple of times to myself. I could not help it, but in that very moment I just wanted to burst forth in praise to God.

Max and I sat down on the sidewalk. Yes, right there in the middle of the sidewalk. I did not care what the neighbors thought. After all, God had just given us front-row seats to the sunset of the evening. I was not about to miss the opportunity to enjoy this incredible view. For the longest time, Max and I sat in silence, both of us watching God's handiwork before us. And then I began to praise!

A bazillion different items of praise to God came to my mind: who God is; what He had done for me that day; all the different things I enjoy; thanks for God's provision, for the health and strength given to me from God, for my home and the luxuries in it for me to enjoy, for the food on my table and the cupboards and fridge loaded with more, for family and friends and new people that I meet every day. On and on my list of praise went as Max and I sat there on the sidewalk. Each phase of that sunset gave me another reason to praise God. Not only is God's handiwork awesome, but He is awesome as well! And as the psalmist reminds me, His name is worthy to be praised!

I want to stop my story right there and ask you a couple of questions.

When was the last time you paused from your busyness to simply sit down and enjoy a sunset? When was the last time you burst forth in praise because you simply could not help it? God gives us opportunities to do that every single day. Do we take the opportunity laid out before us?

Then I thought about what my praise is worth to God. God gives me the opportunity to praise Him. Whenever

I choose to take that opportunity and begin to praise, something begins to happen within me.

1. I am silent before God (that is such a good place to be!).
2. Words of praise rise within my heart and begin to come forth from my lips.
3. There is a sense of peace that surrounds me as my own heart and spirit take flight.
4. In that moment, God allows me to see Him as He is, and I feel super blessed and peaceful in His presence. God uses that opportunity to change something within me.

But I want to know, what does that moment do for God? As I sat there enjoying the front-row seat to God's handiwork, I genuinely believed that a smile broke out upon His face. After all, His child was taking a moment to spend some time with Him. Me-and-God time—what could be better than that? That has got to make God happy, right?

I am almost certain that God was smiling down on Max and me as we sat there in His presence on the sidewalk, watching the sun set in the sky. And in that very moment, something else was happening. As I began to lift my words of praise to God's ears, He was exalted! Praise words exalt our great God! They lift Him higher and higher! I began to realize anew that I have one marvelously great and powerful and awesome God!

Something else happens with God as He listens to the praise of His child. He takes great delight in what is being said. "Let them praise His name ... Let them sing praise to Him ... For the Lord takes pleasure in His people" (Psalm 149:3-4).

I tell you, God was smiling!

"Come on, Max," I finally said as I stood up, tugging on his leash, "it's getting dark out here. We'd better go home."

Our walk back to the house was light. My heart was rejoicing. The praise just kept coming. And I realized, once again, through a beautiful evening sunset, just how blessed I am to personally know this great God. Praise the Lord!

Just the Name of Jesus

O Lord my God, I cried out to You, and You heard
me. O Lord, You brought my soul up from the
grave; You have kept me alive, that I should not
go down into the pit ... I cried out to You, O Lord;
and to the Lord I made supplication ... Hear, O
Lord, and have mercy on me; Lord, be my helper!
—Psalm 30:2-3, 8, 10

We have all been in the midst of difficult situations or
been involved in circumstances that are out of our control.
Whether we are dealing with health issues, family issues,
relationship issues, marital issues, job issues, financial
issues, church issues—whatever it is that has blindsided
us—we are not alone. We often feel alone, frustrated,
overwhelmed, out of control, lonely, scared, and uncertain
of how it will all work out. We cry, we shout, we scream, we
talk, and we pray. But when we pray, so often, in the midst
of our difficulties, we may not always know what to say. Can
anyone relate to all that?

Well, in that moment of not knowing what to say, might
I suggest saying just one word. That is all—just one word.

Whenever you are in a situation or a set of circumstances
and you do not know what to say, just say, "Jesus!" The
mere mention of His name will bring His power into every
situation. When you say, "Jesus!" you have His listening

ear. You really do not need to say another word. "Jesus" is enough! He already knows every detail of what is going on in your life at the very moment you cry out to Him. He knows what your heart is feeling, and He understands every emotion you are experiencing.

"Jesus!" Just one word. It opens the door for His coming to you, ready to help and comfort you. It opens the door for His power, wisdom, love, comfort, and everything else that you need to be yours in that moment. It opens the door for God's Son, Jesus, to do a mighty work both in your personal life and in your circumstances. Jesus can heal your heart's wound. Jesus can intervene and help bring about resolution. Jesus can provide everything that you have need of. Jesus can bring peace, calm, comfort, grace, and love into whatever set of circumstances you are in. Try it. Just call out His name, that wonderful name: "Jesus!"

The psalmist cried out to the Lord, his God. He needed God's help so he would not go deeper into the pit. He needed deliverance from his enemies. We do not need to know all the details of his situation. No one needs to know yours. But there is one who is waiting for you to cry out. Just say one word: "Jesus!"

Jesus met the psalmist right at his point of need. His cries were heard. Help was given. And in the end, the psalmist could praise the Lord, his God: "I will extol You, O Lord, for You have lifted me up, and have not let my foes rejoice over me ... You have turned for me my mourning into dancing; You have put off my sackcloth and clothed me with gladness, to the end that my glory may sing praise to You and not be silent. O Lord my God, I will give thanks to you forever" (Psalm 30:1, 11-12).

Can One Book Really Change Your Life?

One book can change a life forever! Yes! It can!

I remember a time I visited an outdoor book sale. Now, you have to know this truth about me: I am a sucker for books! Just ask my husband. I can (and often do!) spend hours at a time in a bookstore. I easily get lost in the world of books.

So it really was not one bit surprising that I was drawn into this outdoor book sale. I was ever so eager to check out what books they were offering. But after a quick perusal of all the books, I decided that this particular book sale was not for me.

As I turned to leave, a woman a little older than I stopped me and said, "Are you not going to buy any of our books today?" I glanced up at her, smiled, and graciously said, "I'm sorry, but I don't think so. Not today."

"Well, are you looking for something in particular? Maybe I can help you find something here that would interest you," she replied, trying her best to encourage that second look around. I told her that I was in search for some Bibles.

With that word, "Bibles," her eyes got wide, and her voice raised a few decibels. "What? You want a Bible! Whatever for? Bibles are so outdated and worthless. Who in their right mind would want one of those?"

Okay, now I really knew I did not want to be at this book

sale. I was not up for a debate that day—not with this lady. So I smiled graciously, turned, and walked away.

Later I thought of a million different things that I could have said and perhaps should have said. I am so glad that I held my tongue. But the experience did one thing for me. It solidified in my own heart what I think about the Bible. Yes, the Bible has been around for a very long time. There is many an old Bible lying around in peoples' homes and in churches, just waiting to be read. The Bible has been written in many different languages so people groups all over the world, through many generations, may read the Bible and learn more about God.

As to it being outdated, well, I would have to disagree with that one. I find, through reading the words within its pages, that the Bible is still relevant and applicable for life today. There are many worthwhile things to read about within its pages.

And then, as to the Bible being worthless, I guess that depends upon the eye of the beholder. Personally, I do not find that the Bible is one bit worthless. Bibles are precious to me because God is precious to me!

Because I have a personal relationship with God, I treasure every word that He has written within the pages of the Bible. Reading those words, to me, is like going on a journey of discovery, searching for something precious, and finding rare gems of great worth. To me the Bible is a priceless treasure. It is the greatest book ever written, in my opinion.

Even David, one of many writers of God's Word, thought the Bible was something special. David wrote often about the Word of God. One of my favorites among those writings is Psalm 19:7–9, where he describes the Bible (God's Word). Here is what he says: "The law of the Lord is perfect, converting the soul; the testimony of the Lord is sure, making wise the simple; the statutes of the Lord are right, rejoicing the heart; the commandment of the Lord is pure, enlightening the eyes; the fear of the Lord is clean, enduring forever; the judgments of the Lord are true and righteous altogether."

The words "law," "testimony," "statutes," "commandments," "fear," and "judgments" are all synonyms for God's Word, the Bible. David describes the law as perfect, the testimony as sure, the statutes as right, the commandments as pure, the fear as clean, and the judgments as true and righteous. Those are some descriptive words that David uses. How can anyone say that those things are not relevant for today? Do we not look for those things in life today? They were relevant in David's time, and I certainly believe that they are relevant for my time now.

David not only describes God's Word for us but also shares his reaction to it. Let's look at verses 10-11: "More to be desired are they than gold, yes, than much fine gold; sweeter also than honey and the honeycomb. Moreover, by them Your servant is warned, and in keeping them there is great reward."

God's Word was valuable to David—a priceless treasure for sure! To him it was desired more than the finest and purest of gold. It was the sweetest thing ever to enjoy. And to him there was great reward in spending time reading and listening to the words of God. It is a reward that waits for you too—a reward from God that is given only when you open the pages of your own Bible and begin to read.

And I know, speaking from years of reading experience in the Bible, that God's Word is worthy of a good read. It is relevant enough and powerful enough to make major changes in the life of any reader. I know because God's Word has changed my life!

There is one more thing that I would really like for you to see from these Bible verses in Psalm 19. David shares nine things that God's Word can do in the life of the one who reads it, who delights in it, who yearns to believe it, and who seeks to obey it. Following are these nine wonderful ways in which simply reading the Bible can change your life.

- God's Word can redeem your soul, "converting the soul" (Psalm 19:7). This means that it can bring salvation to you. Through the Bible, the reader can learn of God's gift of salvation, which is freely given to all who believe.
- God's Word can renew your mind, "making wise the simple" (Psalm 19:7). Great wisdom from an Almighty God is found within the pages of the Bible.
- God's Word can rejoice your heart: "... rejoicing the heart" (Psalm 19:8). God's Word brings joy, and it is the kind of joy that no one can take away from you.
- God's Word can refocus your vision, "enlightening the eyes" (Psalm 19:8). God's Word will change your focus on things. The more you read, the more clearly you will see the truth.
- God's Word can refresh your life, "enduring forever" (Psalm 19:9). God's Word is designed to bring new life into those who believe in God—a life that will endure forever with God in heaven.
- God's Word can replace your doubts: "... true and righteous altogether" (Psalm 19:9). When things that are true and righteous exist together, there is no room for doubts. The reading of God's Word on a consistent basis removes our doubts. In its place, God instills trust—trust in Him.
- God's Word can reorder your values: "... more to be desired are they than gold" (Psalm 19:9). Who does not want great riches in their life? As you spend more time in God's Word, you begin to realize that you hold in your hands a priceless treasure that is

worth more than the purest gold that the world has to offer you.

- God's Word can redirect your steps: "… moreover by them Your servant is warned" (Psalm 19:11). God's Word holds within its pages many a warning for those who want to follow God. As we listen to those warnings and take heed of them, the pathway we walk becomes clearer. Sometimes God, through warning, will take us off one pathway and put us on a completely different path for life. That is God redirecting our steps away from danger and pointing us toward that which is good.

- God's Word rewards your obedience: "… and in keeping them there is great reward" (Psalm 19:11). Whenever we choose to read the Bible, listen to what God says in it, and choose to meditate upon the very words of God and seek to obey them, God tells us there is "great reward" awaiting us. God rewards our obedience to His Word.

So, I must ask, just one more time: can one book really change your life?

Finding Treasure

But my heart stands in awe of Your
Word. I rejoice at Your Word as
one who finds great treasure.
—Psalm 119:161–162

God's Word is like a giant treasure trove! It is just bursting forth with the best-ever treasures that one could ask for or hope to find. All that treasure is right there for the taking. But you will not really know what is there until you start digging. Dig hard, dig long, and dig deep and you will surely find something precious and valuable.

For years now, I have been teaching kids about the treasures found in God's Word, the Bible. I tell them that it is kind of like a game of hide-and-seek. God has hidden within the pages of His Word special treasures that He wants to share with His children. They are hidden in secret places, and we will not know what they are until we begin to seek after them. The Father invites His children to come "seek out those treasures I have left for you." With a keen excitement and joyful anticipation, we should go and seek out those special treasures left by our heavenly Father. "Seek and you will find," He promises (Matthew 7:7). With a loving heart and a watchful eye, the Father awaits that gleeful shout from one of His children: "I found it!"

So what kinds of treasure do we find within the pages of His Word? Oh, there are so many, many treasures! But here is a brief look at four of them.

God's Love

This is an enormous treasure. It shines so brightly within the pages of God's Word. No one can imagine its height and depth, or its length and width, and no one can strive to reach around it. It never goes away; it never fades from view, and it is guaranteed to never tarnish. God's love is constant, faithful, and totally unconditional. There is enough to go around for all of God's children! Once you find this treasure, you will never be the same. You will want more and more of this great love. In the process of being loved by the Father, you will learn how to love others in the same way. It is a treasure you can claim as your own, and at the same time, it is a treasure that you can pass on, sharing that love with others. "How precious is Your unfailing love, O God" (Psalm 36:7).

Sins Forgiven

This starts out as a dark treasure when it is first found. It is dark as a result of the sin that it contains—your sin, my sin, and the sin of the whole world. The Bible talks about our sin and how we are all sinners in need of a Savior. The Father, God, sent His one and only Son, Jesus, to this earth to bear the punishment of all our sins upon His body. He bled and died upon the cross to save us from our sins. When we believe in Him and ask for forgiveness of our sins, He will faithfully forgive us our sins and cleanse us from all our iniquity or sin (1 John 1:9). The treasure that we find of sins forgiven may start out dark from the very sin it holds. But when we seek for and find that precious treasure, then something amazing happens. If we believe, and if we confess our sins to Him, then He will change that dark sinful treasure into something that is whiter than snow. His forgiveness washes us clean. All that sin will be gone. "As far as the east is from the west, so far has He removed our transgression from us" (Psalm 103:12).

Eternal Life

There is a story in the Bible of a rich young man who came to Jesus and asked this question: "What must I do to inherit eternal life?" (Mark 10:17). Great question! It is one that we all should ask. The truth is that eternal life is not something that we will inherit from our parents. It is not something that we can buy, no matter the costly price tag. We cannot even work for it. But God's Word tells us that eternal life is a free gift from God. It comes straight from the Heavenly Father, God, and is freely given to all who will believe on His Son, Jesus. God offers the gift of eternal life to you. Have you accepted that gift? "He asked life from You, and You gave it to him – length of days forever and ever" (Psalm 21:4).

Precious Promises

Within the pages of God's Word are recorded promise after promise from God to His children, each one of which is so very precious and extremely valuable. One could spend their entire lifetime gathering each promise waiting to be claimed. Here is what I have learned of God's promises: they are real and lasting! They are written just for me. They are mine to claim as my own. There are promises for every season of my life. They are something that I can cherish deeply within my heart. They are eternal, and they are never broken. "My covenant I will not break, nor alter the word that has gone out of My lips" (Psalm 89:34).

If we start with just these four treasures found in God's Word, then we are well on our way to building a wonderful trove of treasure from a great God! And yet here is the good news: that is not all the treasure! The rest is waiting for you to come, seek it, and find it within the pages of God's Word, the Bible. May I encourage you to pick up a copy today and start digging! The treasures are waiting, just as promised!

Praising God in the Tough Times

I will praise You with my whole heart; before
the gods I will sing praises to You. I will
worship toward Your holy temple and praise
Your name, for Your lovingkindness and Your
truth; for You have magnified Your word
above all Your name. In the day when I cried
out, You answered me and made me bold with
strength in my soul ... Though I walk in the
midst of trouble, You will revive me; You will
stretch out Your hand against the wrath of
my enemies, and Your right hand will save me.
The Lord will perfect that which concerns
me; Your mercy, O Lord, endures forever.
—Psalm 138:1–8

Life is just tough at times. It can be filled with tough
circumstances to navigate, tough battles to win, tough
problems to pan out, tough choices to choose, tough people
to persuade, tough struggles to solve, tough finances to
find, and tough work to complete. Let's face it; life is tough!
It is not for the lighthearted; that is for sure. So what kind
of toughness is life asking you to deal with at this moment
in time?

Lately I have been asked to walk through at least
a dozen different tough things all at one time. I could

probably think of a few more than a dozen if I really put my mind to thinking. One thing I have learned through my life, though, is that when I am going through the tough stuff of life, I do not have to do it alone. Others are usually around to help me. Be it family, friends, coworkers, neighbors, or even a stranger, usually someone is there to assist. But the one who helps me the most is my God!

God is always with me through the good times and bad times. He is especially present during the tough stuff. He promises, "I will never leave nor forsake you" (Hebrews 13:5), and thus far, in my life, He has totally kept that promise. So I know God will always be there to help me in and through the tough times of life.

Recently, as I was curled up on the sofa, the dog tightly curled up next to me, a cup of hot tea warming my hands, and my Bible lying open across my lap, I was thinking about some of the tough times I had endured of late. I had a really big decision to make. I had a financial deadline to meet. I had some people I wanted to help but was unsure of even how to help them. I had a burden lying heavy on my heart that I turned into a prayer request from my lips to God's listening ears. I had a lot of things to take care of that day—plenty of errands to run, places to go, and people to see. I knew I needed lots of energy for the day if I had any hope of accomplishing everything on my to-do list. But first I needed some alone time with my God. I reached down to my Bible, placing my hand on the bookmark sticking out of its pages. That bookmark held the place where I would pick up my reading for the day: Psalm 138.

I got so excited as I read God's Word. It seemed as though the words on the page were just jumping right out at me, hoping that I would take notice of them.

Notice them I did. Those words were just what I needed to read on this particular morning. For a few moments, I was able to put some tough stuff aside and think about what I had just read. In fact, I read it again. And again. I came away with seven tidbits of encouragement from my God that morning. You see, God was showing me exactly what He wanted to do for me that day, as together we would deal with my tough stuff of life.

God showing me those seven tidbits started with me crying out to God. This is reminiscent of the psalmist: "... when I cried out, You answered me" (Psalm 138:3). God heard my cries for help. And in hearing me, He was ready to help me. So here are the seven tidbits of help and encouragement from my God, taken from my Bible reading as I sat curled up on the sofa on this particular morning.

1. He is ready to answer me! I know that sounds rather simple. That is because it is! God answers me when I talk with Him. When I include Him in the talks through the tough stuff, He listens, He hears, and He answers. That is because He is concerned about me, concerned about what I am going through, and He's concerned about how I am going to handle every situation.

2. He is ready to embolden (encourage) me with strength! Yes, I definitely needed strength on this particular day. My God knew that. He knows everything about me. I knew—boy, did I ever know—that there was no way I was getting through this day in my own strength. I simply would not make it on my own. And so my God offered to give me a portion of His strength. Whew, just the thought of His strength makes me feel stronger.

3. He is ready to revive my fainting, tired soul! I think I am going to need that too. Throughout the day, I can count on my God to revive my very soul, to speak His peace into it so that I do not grow tired and faint-hearted. He will revive me as I take refuge in Him.

4. He is ready to stretch forth His powerful right hand and deal with my enemies! Wow! I am really glad that my God never leaves me alone with my enemies, or else who knows what might happen. That is also encouraging to me, because while I might not know how best to handle my enemies, my God knows just what to do. I think I will leave that battle to Him.

5. He is ready to save me with His right hand! That same powerful right hand He uses to fight my enemies and my battles for me is the same powerful right hand He uses to save me, to rescue me, and to deliver me from harm. My God is the most powerful weapon and the most powerful deliverer all in one. I think I should tap into His power a little more.

6. He is ready to protect all that concerns me! He is concerned about all those things that I tend to worry about, be fearful over, and seek to control and fix on my own, and He assists me in dealing with them. So God seeks to protect all my family and friends whom I am concerned about too. What concerns me concerns my God. And when I need protection, He will protect. What a comforting thought that is.

7. He is ready to show me that His mercy and His lovingkindness endure forever! He has shown me that so many other times in my life, but I forget. I am so glad that God wants to remind me of this time and time again.

I look over those seven tidbits of help, and I am greatly encouraged because I realize that my God has me covered. He will be with me. He stands ready to help me in and through whatever tough time I face on any given day.

Would you like to know what the psalmist David did when he realized that same truth? He began to praise his God. David praised with his whole heart before others and toward God's holy temple. David praised his God. He praised His name, His lovingkindness, His truth, and His Word. David praised his God.

And in that moment of truth, as God's lesson that morning worked its way from my head down to my heart, I, too, wanted to praise my God. I praised His name, His lovingkindness, His truth, and His Word. But I also praised Him for answering my prayer and reminding me once again that He, my powerful, almighty God, would carry me through another tough day. Together we would do the tough stuff. And at the end of the day, I would be able to praise Him all over again. I "shall sing of the ways of the Lord, for great is the glory of the Lord" (Psalm 138:5).

Putting On My Spiritual Specs

Make a joyful shout to God, all the earth! Sing
out the honor of His name; make His praise
glorious. Say to God, how awesome are Your
works! Through the greatness of Your power
Your enemies shall submit themselves to
You. All the earth shall worship You and sing
praises to You; they shall sing praises to Your
name. Come and see the works of God; He is
awesome in His doing toward the sons of men.
—Psalm 66:1-5

Those of you who have to wear glasses will no doubt relate to this story. If anything, it might just provide a little chuckle.

What are glasses? Glasses are those necessary aids that enhance our vision. Glasses enable us to see the world more clearly (literally!). Glasses help bring clarity and correctness to the things we look at every day. Glasses help us read a good book or watch a sunset in vivid color. They enable us to see where we are going when driving. Glasses are those things we often look for, only to find them on the top of our heads. Glasses are an option for some, while they are an absolute necessity for others. Glasses are the thing that some of us just cannot live without!

I personally have worn glasses from the time I was a

young girl. My mother would tell the story that she finally realized I needed glasses when I kept running into the walls at home. I remember those days—and the bumps and bruises that went along with those wall encounters. Not fun!

I also remember the first time I went to the eye doctor, with Mom assuring me that it was not going to hurt one bit. For some weird reason, the eye chart fascinated me. I asked the doctor, after he finished having me read the line that I could see the clearest, "What line did I read? Point me to it." Bless his heart, he humored me and pointed to the exact line that I had read out loud to him. Not bad. Then I said—rather bravely of me, I thought—"When do I get to go to the top of the chart?" Well, hey, before you start laughing at me, you must give credit to a kid that wanted to move up in the world. That doctor gazed at me with the strangest look on his face. I did not understand. Then he looked at my mom, and for some reason they were both laughing. Hmm, did they know something that I did not? Then he looked back at me, and with a smile on his face, he said, "My dear little girl, this is one chart that you don't want to climb. At least not anytime soon!"

Now I understand what that doctor meant. "Please, sir, can I go back down to the bottom of the chart? Please!"

Nowadays I am totally lost without my glasses. They are, and have been for years, a permanent fixture on my face. I do not ever leave home without them. I do not even roam around in my house without them. If I tried, I would be guaranteed to hit those walls again. My glasses are the first thing I put on in the morning and the last thing I remove at night. And nobody had better touch my glasses while I sleep.

Recently I had an experience with my glasses that … well, use your imagination here. You will get it.

It was during the wee hours of the morning that I woke

up with a start. I am not sure whether I heard something, had a nightmare, or it was just one of those sleepless nights. But I was awake. I lay there in the darkness for what seemed to be ages. It was dark in that room. Normally I like that, but not on this night. It kind of had a creepy feel to it, though I'm not sure why. It was clear that sleep was done for me. As I lay there, my brain switched on like a lightbulb, bright, bold, and beautiful. I love my mind, but not at three o'clock in the morning. I decided to get up. I rolled over and reached for my glasses.

"What? ... Where?"

Panic hit my heart. I know this because it started pounding in my chest pretty hard! I was trying my best not to fall out of the bed. And I was being ever so careful not to waken the hubby lying next to me. I especially did not want to wake up the dog, who was lying in his own bed on the floor next to my bed. If Max heard me, that was it. I would have to get up for sure. But I could not find my glasses!

Who took my glasses? Where are they? My hand was flying all over that nightstand. *They were just here. This is where I left them. But, for some strange reason, they are not there now.* Suddenly, I heard the whimper. *Yep! Max is awake. Good night, nighttime! Good very early morning, Max!*

Before I knew it, I was on the floor. *Please, do not let me step on my glasses.* That would be all I needed. I was down on the floor, hands and knees knocking everywhere, trying my best to feel my way around in the dark. Of course, Max was thinking it was playtime, and he quite happily offered to help with the search. *Where, oh where, are my glasses? Do not panic! You will find them. Oh good, hubby is still snoring! Long may that continue, as I do not want to wake him up.* I still cannot find my glasses! "No, Max, I am not playing! Not now." It is a horrible feeling when you have to get up in the middle of the night and you cannot find your glasses!

Max and I finally gave up the search. Both of us

exhausted from the search, we lay down on the rug on the floor and went to sleep. Hubby never knew! Or did he?

In the morning, when the alarm went off, I reached up onto the nightstand by my bed. Lo and behold, I found my glasses right there—right where I had left them!

All day long, I chuckled to myself over that story as it played out in my mind. How crazy! With a little sleep and a good pair of glasses, it is amazing what you can see! What was lost is now found!

I realized that day something spiritual about glasses. Yes, there really is a spiritual lesson here.

God gave to humankind the ability to read written words. And He provided us with His written word, the Bible. Many of us own a copy of the Bible. Some might even have multiple copies and different versions of the Bible. But the Bible will do us no good at all if we just leave it on a bookshelf or a table somewhere in the house. In order to know what it says, we should open it and read it. Within its pages we will learn about God, about heaven, about God's Son, Jesus, and so much more.

Once we open that Bible to read, many of us will reach for our glasses (or spectacles, as some call them—"specs" for short). Why do we need our glasses? Well, we need them for the simple reason that we want to be able to see what it is we are reading. We want to see the written word more clearly.

And yet when it comes to reading the Word, we tend to be blind. We cannot see it very well at all. It is a little blurry, and we lack perception. Everything seems to run together into a great big blur. The understanding of what we are looking at is just not there. We are blind without some help in our seeing.

In a sense, we need to put on our "spiritual glasses" to be able to see and understand the good things that God wants us to read and to know from within the pages of His Word.

So the next time you sit down to read the Bible, God's Word to you, put on your spiritual glasses—your SPECS, if you will. And as you read, ask yourself these questions:

S: Is there a particular *sin* mentioned that I should avoid?

P: Is there a *promise* that I can claim as God's special promise just for me?

E: Is there someone's good *example* that I can learn from and follow?

C: Is there a *command* from God to obey—something that God expects me to do or be?

S: Is there anything *special* that I should know about God or His Son, Jesus?

Asking yourself these questions is guaranteed to open the eyes of your understanding. And it will help you see things just a little more clearly.

With the right pair of glasses, you will be able to see, like the psalmist, the works of God so clearly. You will, with the psalmist, be able to sing and shout out, in honor of His name, "How awesome are Your works!" (Psalm 66:3).

With the right pair of glasses, you will see "He is awesome in His doing toward the sons of men" (Psalm 66:5).

Now, where did I put those glasses?

Strength for the Battle

I will love You, O Lord my strength. The Lord
is my rock and my fortress and my deliverer;
my God, my strength, in whom I will trust;
my shield and the horn of my salvation, my
stronghold. I will call upon the Lord, who is
worthy to be praised; so, shall I be saved
from my enemies ... In my distress I called
upon the Lord and cried out to my God; He
heard my voice from His temple, and my
cry came before Him, even to His ears.
—Psalm 18:1–3, 6

What kind of battle are you facing today?

Each and every day, we all face a battle of some kind or another in our personal lives. The reality is that battles are a fact of life. It is through those battles that we build our characters, find our strengths, learn who has our backs, and step out in courage to fight another day. What kind of battle are you engaged in today?

- A battle at home? At work? On a foreign field?
- A battle of health issues? With medical doctors?
- A battle of finances? Trying to clear debt? Attempting to earn extra money to pay the bills?

- A battle of homeownership? Trying to keep up with your mortgage payments?
- A battle of homelessness? Attempting to find a safe place? Trying to find the next meal?
- A battle with the children? Stubborn wills? Defiant behavior? Annoying attitudes?
- A battle with the family? Marriage troubles? Relationship with the in-laws? Arguments with the siblings?
- A battle for employment? Finding the right job? Keeping your job?
- A battle of war? Deployed on the battlefield? Helping to keep the peace in a war-torn country?
- A battle of the mind? Striving to maintain mental stability?
- A battle of spiritual proportion? God's will vs. your own will? Conflict with Satan?
- A battle of_____? What is your battle?

There are so many different battles in life. Every day, we engage in one type or another. Sometimes we can choose these battles, and other times we are thrown into the depths of battle without even realizing it.

The psalmist David was ever so familiar with battles. Even before he was a king, David faced battles. As a shepherd, he battled for the safety of his sheep against lions and bears that sought to devour his precious fold. As a young man, he stood up against a nine-foot giant named Goliath and did battle with just a sling and five smooth stones. The Lord was on his side to help him fight that giant, and David knocked him dead with one powerful blow. David battled the threats and attempts of King Saul, who desired to kill him out of jealousy. He ran for his very life as opposed to engaging in face-to-face conflict with him. As a king, he would lead his men into battle against other kings and nations. David knew all about battles. He suffered the consequences of some. And he rejoiced in the victory of many.

Psalm 18 is a record of David's response when God provided deliverance from his enemies after a time of battle with them. Written to the chief musician, this is the "Psalm of David, the servant of the Lord, who spoke to the Lord the words of this song on the day that the Lord delivered him from the hand of all his enemies and from the hand of Saul" (Psalm 18:1).

In the midst of his battles, David had learned this: He needed God! He needed God to be with him in battle, to strengthen him, to protect him, to give him wisdom, and to bring him victory. Hmm, don't we need that in our battles as well? I know I sure do. And thus, God can be that for us as well.

David starts out this Psalm by giving praise to God. David gives tribute to the Lord, who was his strength, his rock, his fortress, his deliverer, his shield, his horn, and his stronghold. David says that his God is "worthy to be praised" (Psalm 18:3b). David received help from his God in the midst of battle. His help came from the Lord, his God. And David was grateful.

So how did David get that help? Simple. He called upon the Lord! "In my distress, I called upon the Lord, and cried out to my God" (Psalm 18:6). Whenever we are in the midst of our own battles, no matter what kind of battle it is, and no matter where that battle is taking place, we, too, can call out to the Lord, our God. We can cry out for strength in the midst of our battles. We can know that God is on our side.

Was God on David's side? Absolutely! "He heard my voice from His temple and my cry came before Him, even to His ears" (Psalm 18:6b). God hears when we cry out to Him. He knows about our battles. He sees them. He allows them to take place in our lives. But in the midst of our battles, He is there for us. He stands ready to help. He is listening for our cries. He hears, and He will answer. His strength will become our strength. He will help fight the battle with us. He will bring about victory in His perfect time and in His way. That is the Lord, our God!

As I read on in this psalm of David, I learned something else that really blessed my heart. David shares some of the things that God did for him in the midst of the battle. And I love the way David says it. I love the words he used. The help and encouragement that David received from the hand of the Lord, his God, was breathtakingly beautiful. Try reading David's words out loud. You can almost hear his voice as he describes the Lord's help in the midst of the battle.

The Lord thundered from heaven. (Psalm 18:13)

He sent out His arrows and scattered the foe. (Psalm 18:14)

He took me, drew me out of many waters. He delivered me from my strong enemy. (Psalm 18:16-17)

The Lord was my support. (Psalm 18:18)

He delivered me because He delighted in me. (Psalm 18:19)

For by You I can run against a troop, by my God I can leap over a wall. (Psalm 18:29)

He is a shield to all who trust in Him. (Psalm 18:30)

It is God who arms me with strength and makes my way perfect. (Psalm 18:32)

He makes my feet like the feet of a deer and sets me on my high places. (Psalm 18:33)

He teaches my hands to make war so that my arms can bend a bow of bronze. (Psalm 18:34)

You have also given me the shield of salvation; Your right hand has held me up; Your gentleness has made me great. You enlarged my path under me, so my feet did not slip. (Psalm 18:35-36)

You have armed me with strength for the battle. (Psalm 18:39)

I do not know about you, but when I read through that list, my heart does flip-flops! There is no doubt whatsoever that God was present with David in the midst of his battle. And no doubt, whenever David cried out to God, He was there for David. God provided David all that he needed to be successful in battle.

It is no wonder that David wrote a psalm of praise to the God of the battles. This is David's praise: "The Lord lives! Blessed be my Rock! Let the God of my salvation be exalted … Therefore, I will give thanks to You, O Lord, among the Gentiles, and sing praise to Your name" (Psalm 18:46, 49).

For myself, I realize, once again, that when I am in the midst of battle of any kind, I, too, can call out to God, and He will come to me and give me aid in that battle. My strength and help will come from Him. The wisdom I need to make good decisions in the battle will be His wisdom. He will be my rock, my fortress, and my deliverer. And for that, I, too, can give praise to my God.

Let's go back to my first question. What kind of battle are you facing today? Have you cried out yet to the only one who has your back? He is listening for that battle cry!

Finding My Rest

Rest in the Lord and wait patiently for Him.
—Psalm 37:7

Rest! What a blissfully sweet word! Just mention the word "walk" and the ears on our little dog, Max, spring right up. The excitement is more than he can contain! I do not usually have to say the word a second time. In his eagerness to get started, he races through the house. If he could talk, I am almost certain that I would hear him say, "Hurry up and get my harness and leash on me!" He is ready to go for a w-a-l-k!

On one particular morning, Max and I went out for a walk. I am telling you, this dog loves his walks! Every walk holds a new adventure for him and for the person who is hanging onto the leash. He stops often just to take in the sights and sounds around him. He is busy poking his little nose into just about every nook and cranny along the way. He has a friendly greeting for every person he meets along the path. That tail-wagging greeting is the best thing-ever to brighten up my day! And then there are all the stops at the houses where his "friends" live. A quick little bark to say hello, and we are off walking again. Today he was especially interested in chasing the birds. It seems he is listening for their special song, and when he hears it, he stops and assesses where it is coming from. Should he have the pleasure of seeing the bird, well, that is when the real fun begins. *Catch me if you can!* I am thankful he has never actually caught one yet. But he certainly gives it his best try. The birds are always quick to fly away.

Today I almost lost my grip on his leash when he unexpectedly lunged after a rabbit. I did not see that one coming. I am not sure who was more surprised—the rabbit or me. Perhaps Max thought that cute little rabbit was lunch, but happily the rabbit was not interested in Max and quickly disappeared out of sight. Max let out a little growl of disappointment. Poor Max!

A little while later, a big gust of wind caught him totally off guard, and he began nipping at it. I chuckled at the thought of trying to catch the wind. *As if you really could, Max.* I tell you, walking with this dog is a new experience every day. And yet I must admit, when I think about it, there are plenty of life lessons to learn from walking my dog.

For the first time ever, today on our walk, Max got tired out! I mean the totally exhausted kind of tired! It is not really that surprising though. Worn out by the adventure, he plopped himself down right in the middle of the sidewalk. He refused to move.

"Really, Max? You have to stop right here? Right now?"

At least he had picked a shady spot to sit down in. I was afraid he was down for the count. He let out the cutest, most exhausted sigh that I have ever heard from my dog. No amount of tugging on the leash, no amount of petting, no amount of "That's a good boy!" and certainly no amount of promised treats, nothing—I repeat, nothing—was going to entice him to move forward and finish our walk. Nothing!

At first he just sat there looking all around him. I was trying to figure out what he was watching. What was it that he might be preparing to go after next? But there was nothing—nothing that I could see anyway.

All of a sudden, instead of sitting, Max lay down on the cool, shady sidewalk and spread out all four legs. One, two, three, and four! Then he dropped his head, allowing another sigh to escape. He closed his eyes. Nope, he was definitely not moving. He was totally exhausted! It was time to rest!

What was his favorite dog-walker to do?

In that moment, I simply chose to sit down with my favorite dog on the sidewalk and take a rest. I know, I could have picked him up and carried him back home. But why? It was a lovely day. And while I was out walking my dog, Max unknowingly taught me a very simple yet valuable life lesson. Sometimes we just need to stop and rest!

Life can be extremely hectic. Very often we find life to be fast paced and super busy. We tend to always be on the run, with places to go, people to see, things to do, deadlines to meet, and dreams to fulfill. Life can be filled with many challenges, many problems. Many things we seem to chase after, many different dramatic scenarios, and occasionally comedy play out day by day. All too often, there is something or someone "tugging at our leash" to keep us from moving forward. Let's get this thing called life done. Let's finish our walk.

But sometimes we just need to stop where we are, stop what we are doing, lie down, and rest!

Rest is a gift that we can give to ourselves in the midst of our very hectic lives. My dog, Max, reminded me of that little lesson today, out on our walk together. Rest is good. Rest is necessary. Rest is restorative to our bodies, souls, and minds. Rest is not idle. It is not wasteful time. Sometimes rest is the most productive thing we can do in a day. We all need rest!

I would like to share with you four things that I have learned about rest.

Rest gives me the opportunity to retreat. I love that word, "retreat." It means "to pull away from something or someone for a designated period of time. To separate from something to rest and relax." It is that idea of stopping one or more actions in life for a time to concentrate on something else. I have learned to schedule times of retreat into my life. If I do not intentionally schedule them, then they usually do not happen at all.

I look forward to my times of retreat. I intentionally put my work aside. Yeah, no housework! No laundry! No fixing of meals (they get done ahead of time)! At my personal retreat, there are no people, no problems, and thus no potential disturbances. During many of my times of retreat, I intentionally retreat from technology, and so, no phones, no computers, and no television will be allowed at my retreat. It's just me and quiet! It is best for me to retreat somewhere away from home, and thus away from temptations to rush back into life's complicated chaos. When I am away from home, I cannot pick up my personal baggage of life or my work and bring it into my retreat space. My retreats can last for a few hours, a full day, or even for several days—whatever I deem my retreat to be. Sometimes my retreat will include a good, well-deserved nap. Retreat, for me, is all about rest. I rest from the normal pace of life; from my work; from technology, which zaps so much of my time and energy; and from my worries and concerns, resting my body, soul, and mind.

Rest gives me the opportunity to enter God's presence. Pulling away from the demands of life, pulling away from responsibilities, and pulling away from everything else gives me the privilege of retreating with my Creator God. It is an opportunity to come into His sacred presence and just dwell there with Him. I am able to enter and enjoy His presence fully. I do not bring anything else with me. It is just me and my God! It is quiet in His presence. It is so peaceful, and there is no one else to disturb us. His presence brings calm to my tired, troubled heart. In His presence, I can lay down everything: my hurts, my pain, my anxiety, my concerns, and my fears. Everything I have and everything I am is His when I am there in His presence. He takes everything from me. I willingly surrender everything to Him. I can completely, totally, and fully rest in His presence. I can have that long overdue nap while He tenderly watches over His child. In His presence, I can find a special place of refuge. I am safe there in His presence. I can be restored, renewed, and revitalized in my body, soul, and mind.

Rest gives me the opportunity to spend quality time with my Best Friend, my Lord, my God, and my Savior! Together we choose how best to spend that time. I can spend time talking to Him and tell Him anything that I want to. He will listen intently to my every word. I can spend time listening to Him as He speaks softly and gently to me. I want to listen to His every word. I desire His words to wash over my spirit, and to cleanse and refresh my heart and soul.

My God and I can be silent in the presence of one another. We do not have to feel awkward in that silence. The silence is blissful and beautiful. As we spend time together, I can read His Word out loud. I read His words back to Him, and from the very pages of my Bible, my God speaks to me. I can ask Him questions. He will explain His truths to my open heart and mind. I want to hear only His words in this special time together. I can worship Him. There will be no fear that my worship is not good enough, is not pure enough, or is not worthy for Him. I desire my worship to be heartfelt and holy. I want my worship to be glorious to the ears of my Savior. In that worship, I want to sing to Him. I have no worries about making a "joyful noise," for my worship will be beautiful in His presence. As I spend this special, sacred time with my God, my Savior, I will find that true rest comes flooding over my body, soul, and mind.

Rest gives me the opportunity to trust my God. As I am resting in His presence and as I am spending quality time with Him, I loosen my grip on everything else. There is no baggage. There are no problems. There are no fears or doubts. There is nothing that comes between me and my Savior, God. As I rest, everything else fades from view. I have found my place of refuge. I am receiving His refreshment. I am seeing my heart being renewed right before my eyes. I am learning to totally trust the work that my God is doing in these moments of retreats and rest. His work is good. No, it is better than good; it is awesome! It is perfect! It is complete! I am learning to trust Him! My trust grows bigger, deeper, and fuller with every moment we spend together. It is more precious than ever before. I want to trust even more. I want to trust Him with my body, soul, and mind.

Sometimes we just need to stop and rest!

What an Excellent Name

O Lord, our Lord, how excellent is Your name
in all the earth, who have set Your glory above
the heavens! Out of the mouths of babes and
nursing infants You have ordained strength,
because of Your enemies, that You may silence
the enemy and the avenger. When I consider
Your heavens, the work of Your fingers, the
moon, and the stars, which You have ordained,
what is man that You are mindful of him, and
the son of man that You visit him? For You
have made him a little lower than the angels,
and You have crowned him with glory and
honor. You have made him to have dominion
over the works of Your hands; You have put
all things under his feet, all sheep and oxen –
even the beasts of the field, the birds of the
air, and the fish of the sea that pass through
the paths of the seas. O Lord, our Lord, how
excellent is Your name in all the earth.
—Psalm 8:1-9

What is in a name?

A name is so much more than just a name! A name reflects
a place of origin. It indicates a culture, an inheritance
within that origin. Hidden within every name is a special
meaning. You might have been named after someone special

within your family—for example, a grandparent, an aunt or uncle. Perhaps you were given a name that was passed down throughout the family over several generations. It is possible that your parents gave you the name of someone in the Bible, with the hope that you would take on the characteristics of that person in your own life. Your parents might have given you a name that would remind them of someone or something special in their own lives, such as a hero, a favorite singer, a movie star, or an athlete. I have a friend who was named after someone who had saved her mother's life. Another friend of mine was named for a cartoon character. You cannot imagine the teasing that he got all throughout his life. Names are important. They need to be chosen carefully and with some respect to the meaning that that name holds.

In chapter 8 of the book of Psalms, David writes about the name of the Lord. He says not once, but twice, in the nine verses of this chapter, "O Lord, our Lord, how excellent is Your name in all the earth!"

David declares that the name of the Lord, his God, is an excellent name—the best in all the earth—for that name perfectly describes who the Lord is. There is no doubt when it comes to knowing the meaning of that name.

The first "Lord" refers to Jehovah, the covenant-keeping God—the God who keeps His promises. The second "Lord" refers to the Sovereign One, the one who has not only ability but also authority. With an understanding of the meaning behind the name, we might read this verse this way: "O Lord, our promise-making God, our Lord, the Sovereign One who has the ability and authority to keep His promises, how excellent is Your name in all the earth."

David goes on to tell us why he thinks the name of the Lord is so excellent and why He is worthy of our worship and praise.

First, His name reflects His glory. Verse 1 tells us that

His glory is set above the heavens. His glory is majestic, full of splendor, and abundant in magnificence. The very glory of the Lord, our Jehovah, our Sovereign One, shines from the heavens. It is well worth paying attention to.

Secondly, His name reflects His strength. David marveled at the fact that God uses strength from babies and nursing infants to silence the enemy and the avenger. The idea here is that the Lord has ordained the weak things in our world to shame the strong. (See 1 Corinthians 1:27.)

Thirdly, His name reflects His creation. In verse 3 of Psalm 8, David says, "When I consider Your heavens, the work of Your fingers, the moon and the stars, which You have ordained." All around us, we see the creation, the great handiwork of our Lord God. The heavens and earth truly show forth His ability to create something beautiful.

And lastly, His name reflects His authority. David marveled at the fact that the finite (mortal and weak) man that God created was given dominion (authority) over all that He created. God's creation of man is described by David as one of power and dignity: "You made him a little lower than the angels. You have crowned him with glory and honor. You have made him to have dominion over the works of Your hand and You have put all things under his feet" (Psalm 8:5-6). Man was created to be God's representative on this earth, to take care of the things that God had created. David marveled at that truth and the place of honor that God gave to mankind.

As David considered these things, he realized just how precious the very name of the Lord is. The Lord, our Lord, lives up to His name. He is Jehovah. He is the Sovereign One. His name is excellent in all the earth.

Whenever we stop to consider these same things about the Lord, it should greatly move us toward an expression of our own praise to the majestic, excellent name of our Lord. He is worthy of all our praise! What an excellent name!

Oh, My People

Hear, O My people, and I will admonish you!
O Israel, if you will listen to Me! There shall
be no foreign god among you; nor shall you
worship any foreign god. I am the Lord your
God, who brought you out of the land of Egypt;
open your mouth wide, and I will fill it. But my
people would not heed My voice, and Israel
would have none of Me. So, I gave them over
to their own stubborn heart, to walk in their
own counsels. Oh, that My people would listen
to Me, that Israel would walk in My ways!"
—Psalm 81:9-13

Six words—they captured my attention: "If you will listen to Me!"

These six words from the sacred pages of God's Word, the Bible, captured my attention, calling me to listen. What should I do? What would you do?

Let's face it, listening, *really listening*, is quickly becoming a lost art for many of us. What? Not for you? Well, consider this:

- How well do you listen when your boss is giving you instructions for your new assignment?
- How well do you listen when your child is explaining something that happened at school?

- How well do you listen to your friend when they tell you of their difficult situation?
- How well do you listen when Mom and Dad express how concerned they are for you?
- How well do you listen when God calls your name?

We are all very busy people. I get that truth. Sadly, though, sometimes we are too busy to really listen the way that we should. After all, there are places to go, people to see, things to do, projects to complete, decisions to make, and so forth. I am just too busy to list all the different things that we are busy doing. But the reality is that there are always some things that we need to listen to.

Just the other day, I was sitting out in the garden, chatting on my cellphone with a friend. We were both sharing about our busyness. Both of us, were equally busy in our own ways, with lots of various circumstances happening in our lives. I love what my friend did in the middle of that conversation. All of a sudden, she burst out with a loud voice and said, "Stop! We have to stop this! Do you realize what we sound like?"

At first, feeling a little taken aback, I was not sure what to do. But I smiled, though, for I realized what she was saying.

"Stop for a minute, Kathy," she continued. "Just listen to what is happening around you."

The pause, the silence between us, was rather refreshing! Just to take a precious moment and stop everything else, just to listen—what a novel idea!

She broke the silence first and described the sounds she heard in the coffee shop where she was sitting. Then it was my turn.

I described the sounds of the backyard garden: wind whistling through the big pine tree, birds chirping over on the gate, water dripping off the rooftop, our dog digging in a corner, grunting and growling to himself as he worked. For a moment, I thought I could hear a daffodil grow a little taller.

Ah, the art of listening! It had been a while since I literally just sat and listened. It was comforting. It was refreshing. It did my heart good.

And that precious moment of refreshing quiet and restful sounds is just what the Lord God wants to give to His people. If only we would slow down and take the time to listen. "If you will listen to Me!" He gently whispers. Will we listen to His voice?

It reminds me of the Bible story of Mary and Martha, and their visit from Jesus. (See Luke 10:38–42.) We have in this story such a great contrast between the two sisters. Martha was the busy one, getting everything ready for Jesus's visit. And when He arrived, she was still busy making sure everything was just right. And she was fussing in that busyness. "Lord, do You not care that my sister has left me to serve alone? Tell her to help me," Martha said to Jesus. Can anyone else relate to that kind of busyness? I love Jesus's reply to her. He said, "Martha, Martha, you are worried and troubled about many things" (Luke 10:41). Yet I think Jesus was more concerned about her listening skills than He was about her busyness.

And then there is Mary. Jesus said of her, "Mary has chosen the good part, which will not be taken away from her" (Luke 10:42). So what was Mary doing that was better than Martha's busyness?

"Mary ... sat at Jesus' feet and heard His word" (Luke 10:39). Mary chose to put the busyness aside. To her, it did not matter. What was most important to Mary was listening. She sat at Jesus's feet and listened to His every word.

In that very moment of Jesus's presence in their home, nothing else mattered to Mary. She stopped everything else. She gave Him her undivided attention. She sat, in reverent awe, at His feet. She cherished every word He spoke. She listened. She loved what she was hearing, for Mary loved Jesus. She wanted to be in His presence. She wanted to listen!

"But one thing is needed," Jesus said (Luke 10:42). Mary chose it.

I want to choose it too!

Did God Go Out to Lunch?

Why do you stand afar off, O Lord?
Why do You hide in times of trouble?
—Psalm 10:1

Is there anyone else out there, besides me, that feels at times as though God went out to lunch and left you standing all alone? You know, that feeling that God is not really there—the feeling you get when you pray but He seems silent, when you search for Him but He seems to be hiding, when you go through difficulty but He seems to have left you alone, or when you are overwhelmed with life's happenings but He seems to have gone out to lunch.

Has He really gone out to lunch?

Think about the last overwhelming, difficult circumstance that was going on in your life. Think about that last time you wondered whether God had left you—that time when you thought He had abandoned you, or that time when you felt all alone, helpless, and hopeless. Go ahead and identify your most recent upheaval: the blow you felt, the trauma you endured, the wound you are licking, the diagnosis received. Identify that thing that woke you up from that "everything is going smoothly in life" dream you were having. Are you in that moment?

Did you call out to God at that time? "Where are You,

God? Why have You left me here? How am I supposed to deal with this, God? Are You listening to me, God?"

Did your heart sink as you were thinking that God had left you alone? Were you afraid of going at it by yourself? What if God walked away and went to lunch?

In that moment, you must have felt all alone, powerless in fear, and completely overwhelmed by the circumstances that life just dealt to you. I will admit to you honestly that I know that feeling! I have felt that way too many times to count them. It truly is a horrible feeling!

But let's change our mindset for just a moment. What *if* God skipped lunch that day?

Consider for just a moment, though, that God *was* there in the fullness of that event that devastated your life!

The simple Bible truth is that God *was* there! He is always there!

In the darkest moments of our lives, in the upside-down circumstances that frighten us, in the overwhelming events that leave us feeling alone and abandoned, and in the times when we feel afraid, helpless, and as though all hope seems to be gone, He is there!

He saw the very shape of your crisis. He felt the weight of it as it settled upon your life and crushed your very being. He could hear it as it began to break your heart. He sensed your fears, frustrations, and feelings in that very moment. He was there!

He knew the exact size of the wrecking ball that hit your life with a thud. He felt it as you were knocked to the ground. He understood when your world fell apart. He knew in advance that things in your life might never be the same. He was there!

He knew your heart would be broken. He knew that the phone call would come during breakfast with your friends and would interrupt the laughter among friends. He knew that the car accident would happen that very afternoon. He knew just how your doctor would phrase his diagnosis that needed to be delivered to your listening ears. He was there!

He knew how your boss was going to explain your job away from you. He knew how your arms would tremble as you stood reading that note left by a loved one. He knew what horrid pictures you would discover on your computer screen. He knew who would be standing on the other side of the door when you opened it. He knew the numbing pain you felt as you stood at the graveside. He knew the pain of your circumstances that had just rocked your world. He knew. He was there!

And in the moments of your crisis, there is something else that He knew.

He knew that you needed Him to draw near to you. He knew that you wanted Him to hold you tight and just let you cry. He knew to lovingly wipe away your tears. He knew you wanted Him to take away your fear. He knew that you needed His help and comfort. He knew to be gentle in the words He spoke to you. He knew, in the midst of your pain, that He would whisper to you, "My child, I am right here with you!" He knew!

He knew that when He reminded you of His presence, and when He began to give you His love, His strength, His peace, and His hope, that you would collapse into His arms. He knew that He would offer you a safe place of refuge—a place to abide with Him during the course of the storm that raged in your life. He knew that He would carry you through the circumstances. He knew that He would once again set your feet upon solid ground. He knew!

He knew that it was not lunchtime. In the midst of your darkest moment, He never left you. He was in those circumstances with you. He was waiting for the right moment to speak, to act, to perform that miracle, to provide that blessing, and to bring encouragement. He waited for you to acknowledge His presence with you. He knew. He was there with you!

He knew that His child needed Him. He knew! God knew all about your life event. He knew all about His child.

He knew!

He was there!

He was right there with you!

Hope in God

Why are you cast down, O my soul? And why are you disquieted within me? Hope in God, for I shall yet praise Him for the help of His countenance. O my God, my soul is cast down within me; therefore, I will remember You from the land of the Jordan, and from the heights of Hermon, from the Hill Mizar. Deep calls to deep at the noise of Your waterfalls; all Your waves and billows have gone over me. The Lord will command His lovingkindness in the daytime, and in the night His song shall be with me – a prayer to the God of my life. I will say to God my Rock, 'Why have you forgotten me? Why do I go mourning because of the oppression of the enemy?' As with a breaking of my bones, my enemies reproach me, while they say to me all day long, 'Where is your God?' Why are you cast down, O my soul? And why are you disquieted within me? Hope in God; for I shall yet praise Him, the help of my countenance and my God.
—Psalm 42:5-11

I saw her in the hospital's surgical waiting room. My eyes were drawn to the woman in the corner of the room, sitting alone, crying. I really wanted to go to her right then, but someone was waiting for me—someone who desired to sit with me while my husband was having surgery. This someone could only stay for a little while, as work was calling for her attention. I appreciated the fact that someone loved me enough to come and sit with me so I would not have to sit alone. But still my eyes were drawn to the woman in the corner of the room, sitting alone, crying.

The surgical waiting room was populated with plenty of comfortable chairs, and sets of tables and chairs, many of which were occupied by waiting people. Several televisions within the large space were vying for the attention of those in the room. The noise from them was a little distracting, but then, perhaps those waiting really wanted that kind of distraction. A person could watch the news or, over on the other side of the room, a fitness and health program.

One television had a children's cartoon playing. Two children sat close by, quietly laughing together at what they were watching. I would have enjoyed watching the cartoon with them in an attempt to totally take my mind away from the present circumstances, if only for a few moments. Their laughter made me chuckle to myself.

One man sat all alone by the window, working diligently on a crossword puzzle. There was a family huddled together, sharing memories, laughing at pictures collected on their phones. Right in the middle of the room was a fairly large group of people, circled around two people who were standing in the middle. They were all holding hands and praying together. One young mother sat with her little boy, who could not have been more than seven or eight years of age. She comforted her son in her arms as he softly sobbed, asking, "Is Daddy going to be okay?" Another lady sat reading a book, her face bearing a widening smile. She gave an audible chuckle, obviously responding to what she was reading.

I turned around to see an older couple come into the room. The wife was fussing over her husband, telling him where to sit and stating, "It will be just a few moments before they call you back." I enjoyed the compassionate look of love that the husband gave to his wife as he patted her hand. He gently reassured her, "You are going to be just fine as you wait. I will be in the good hands of my surgery team. We will be back together soon." I smiled at the preciousness of that relationship.

I watched as a volunteer worker came to get a young man whose girlfriend had had surgery and was coming out of the recovery area. "You can come with me, sir. I will take you back to your party, and together you can prepare to take her home."

I suddenly realized that my party was waiting for me. I went over to where she was sitting, hugs were exchanged. I then sat down, and we started talking. But still, my eyes were drawn to the woman in the corner of the room, sitting alone, crying.

It did not seem like that long before a volunteer came for me. "The doctor will meet with you now and tell you how your husband's surgery went. Would you like to follow me?" She led me to a little room where, after a few moments, the doctor came to tell me the details of the surgery and then gave me the assurance, "Everything went well."

Hubby was moved to the recovery room, and I would have some more time to wait. My party excused herself, saying that she had to get to work. We hugged, and I thanked her for the time she had spent waiting with me. I walked back into the main waiting area, and once again my eyes were drawn to the woman in the corner of the room, who was still sitting alone and still crying.

This time I walked right over to her, sat down in the chair beside her, and placed my hand upon her shoulder. "I'm sorry to bother you, but ..." I gently said to her.

Without any hesitation, she welcomed me. "Oh, you are not bothering me," she said as she wiped the tears from her eyes.

I handed her another tissue and said, "I have been watching you for some time but could not come over to you until now. Do you mind if I ask, are you all right?"

With tearstained eyes, she looked me in the face. I could not help but notice just how tired this dear lady appeared. She cleared her throat and introduced herself. I then told her my name and a little something funny about me and hospital waiting rooms. We both laughed. Instantly I felt as if we had known each other forever. The conversation that ensued was precious as two people came together in the beginnings of a new friendship. We were comrades in waiting. Both of us were waiting for our husbands to have their surgeries, spend their time in recovery, and (so we hoped) not have to wait a long time before they were sent to their rooms for the night of observation and care.

In the course of our conversation, my new friend asked me a series of questions. Prior to asking her questions, she had shared that her husband had been ill for a long time and had had many surgeries. This one was "the last hope" of any help for him. My heart just ached for this dear lady as I listened to her story. No wonder she was crying. It just broke my heart that she had to sit there all alone. I wrapped my arms about her. We cried together.

After a few moments, through the tears, the questions began.

"Have you ever felt totally helpless and hopeless? ... Have you ever felt like you were in a very long, dark black tunnel and you wondered if the light would ever be seen again? ... Do you know about hopeless circumstances? That is where I am now, and I do not know what to do. I feel so alone! ... What do you do when you feel hopeless?" ... Do you know about hope? Where does it come from? ... How can I find hope?"

I held her in my arms as her body shook with her sobs.

As I tried to comfort this dear woman in the corner of the room, I began to pray out loud. I prayed for my new friend.

"What are you doing?" she asked as our tearstained faces met.

"I am praying to the God of all hope! I am asking the God that I know, the God who has given me hope in many a dreadful circumstance, to meet you right here in this surgical waiting room. I am asking God to wrap His loving arms around us both and give us comfort, peace, and hope for the situations we both find ourselves in. I am asking God to be your light at the end of the tunnel, to be the one who wipes away all your tears, and to be your source of hope."

She sat silently, looking right at me but not responding. Perhaps she was pondering what I had said. I was hoping that I had not offended her.

Finally she calmly and gently said, "No one has ever prayed for me like that before. Thank you! Is your God really the source of hope? Can you keep praying for me?"

I started praying again, out loud, to the God I know so well, who was listening at that very moment to my heartfelt prayer. God was present in the corner of that surgical waiting room, and He brought comfort and peace to this dear lady. For the next hour, we prayed. We cried. We talked about God, about His great love, about His Son, Jesus Christ, and about hope. Together we talked to God. There was an indescribable preciousness to that conversation— one I will never forget.

The truth of the matter is this: Every one of us is faced with difficult times when we wonder what happened to hope. We might face seasons of disappointment, bouts of depression, periods of despair, and cycles of doubt and questions. These can come as a result of health issues, job losses, financial stresses, family difficulties, relationship battles, or any other major experiences that life likes to throw at us.

We have all been—or will be, at some point in life—in a place where we search for hope. We will be in a place where we wonder what we did wrong, where we question the circumstances, or where we feel as if the tunnel just got very dark. We find ourselves asking, "Where is God now?" or "What happened to hope?"

The psalmist faced a time like that. In Psalm 42:6, we have recorded for us the psalmist's cry to God as he searched for hope. He writes, "O my God, my soul is cast down within me." I can assure you that God heard that cry! We are not told what the circumstances were; we do not really need to know. Yet we can relate, can we not? I know I can. I have been there. Many times I have been in the midst of circumstances when all I could do was cry. I have been in the midst of troubled times when I simply did not know what to do next. I have been in the pit of despair and depression when I was certain that the pit would swallow me whole. I have been in the tunnel when it suddenly went dark—very dark. No glimmer of light was to be seen. There was no hope of it ever shining again. Hopelessness became my shroud. I understand what that feels like.

And yet I craved hope! I needed hope! I had to find hope!

It is within that very moment, that moment of searching for hope, that we can turn to the God of all hope. The psalmist said it well in three simple words: "Hope in God!" God is the source of our hope!

You see, God meets us in the darkness of our circumstances. He knows when we feel all alone. He sees our tears. He hears our cries of anguish. He comforts us with His peace. He is the light at the end of our tunnel. He is our source of hope!

So how do we tap into this source of hope? How can we

bring hope into our difficult circumstances that life throws at us? I would like to suggest four things that will lead us closer to the source of hope.

1. Hang on to what you already know about God and believe that He is with you. God is simply waiting for you to call out to Him. He will be right there with you. In fact, His promise to you is this: "I will never leave you nor forsake you" (Hebrews 13:5). Even if you do not acknowledge His presence, He is there. Even if you cannot talk to Him or do not know what to say, He is there. Even if you have never talked to Him before, He is there. He is there for you. He is your source of hope!

2. Open your heart to the fact that God wants to use your present circumstances (no matter how bad you think they are) for your good and for His glory. Yes, it is true, our bad circumstances in life can be used for good in our lives. It is through the bad, difficult, or hard times of life that we can turn toward God. And that is a really good thing for us to do. It is at these times, that we learn a lot of good lessons, such as character development, dependence upon God, patience, self-control, understanding of others, and forgiveness—and the list goes on. We learn valuable lessons during our difficult circumstances that we could never learn any other way. We can carry these lessons with us throughout the rest of our lives, using them to help us the next time we face difficult circumstances. We can even use the lessons that we learn to help and encourage others who are going through the same kind of difficulty.

    God receives the glory when we allow Him to do His perfect work in our hearts during that time. As we open our hearts to God during our difficult circumstances, He shows us more of who He is and what He can do. Through our open hearts, God is glorified!

3. Pour your heart out to God often in prayer. Learn to talk to God during your difficult times. Talk with Him often. He will always be listening. While He already knows all about your needs and your circumstances, He still takes great delight in hearing from you. Every time you begin to pour your heart out to God in blatant honesty, you open the door for God to do His perfect work in your life, in your heart, and in your circumstances. Every time you begin to pour your heart out to God, you will be reminded of His presence with you. He is there in the peace that comes to your heart. He is there in the people who come alongside you to offer assistance and help. He is there in the provisions that come your way to meet your needs. He is there in every comforting hug, in every word of encouragement, and in every prayer that is offered up on your behalf. Every time you begin to pour your heart out to God in prayer, He is there for you. Allow Him to embrace you with His great love. Receive His love with open arms and a welcoming heart. Embrace the light that He brings to your darkness. Hang on to the hope He offers you!

4. Expect an answer to your prayer, to your cry, to your heartache, and to your search for hope. God will answer! Perhaps He will not always do so in the way or in the manner that you might expect. But He will answer in His perfect timing, in His perfect ways, and in His perfect means. His answer to you will be perfect because the God who is answering is perfect. He is a sovereign God, and He knows what He is doing on your behalf. During your difficult circumstances, you can trust Him. He knows what

He is doing in and through your circumstances. And while you wait for His answer, hang on to the hope that He is offering you!

I saw her in the hospital surgical waiting room. My eyes were drawn to the woman in the corner of the room, sitting alone, crying. The God of all hope met her in that corner. He wiped away her tears!

You, O Lord, Are My Rock

For by You, O Lord, I can run against a
troop, by my God, I can leap over a wall.
As for God, His way is perfect; The word
of the Lord is proven; He is a shield to all
who trust in Him. For who is God, except the
Lord? And who is a rock, except our God?
—Psalm 18:29-31

The battle of life is violently raging around me. It is relentless in its intentional pursuit. Day and night, the frightful and haunting sounds from the battlefield creep in to overwhelm my heart, mind, and soul. They give me no rest. Various enemies, clad with their weapons of warfare, seem to be coming at me from every imaginable angle. From without and within, and often with little warning, they seek to disable, discourage, and even destroy.

Who are these enemies that are coming after me?

- the enemy of sin and evil—my own sin and the sins of others around me
- the enemy of temptation—the good, the bad, and the ugly of it all
- the enemy of persecution—bullying unbelievers that go straight for the spirit within

- the enemy of harsh criticism—words that cut like a sharp knife, leaving wounds that are slow to heal
- the enemy of defeat and discouragement seeking to disarm me
- the enemy of broken relationships—the hardship of saying good-bye
- the enemy of death—walking through the valley of the shadow of death with a beloved friend
- the enemy of failing health—so many doctor visits and tests to do
- the enemy of financial struggle—too little money, too many bills
- the enemy of time—so much to do and so little time to do it all
- the enemy of to-do lists—lists that keep on growing while seemingly little gets done
- the enemy of perfectionism—What? Am I the only one?
- the enemy of _____

All too often, in the midst of this raging battle, it seems as though I am just waiting to hit that proverbial wall with an almighty, hard-hitting thud!

But God!

I love what the psalmist David says about his enemy pursuing him and the proverbial wall that he encountered. "For by You, O Lord, I can run against the troop, by my God I can leap over a wall" (Psalm 18:29). I love the picture that comes to my mind when I read those words.

This psalm was written on the day that David was delivered from his number-one enemy, King Saul. The king relentlessly pursued David, with just one intention—to kill him. Saul's jealousy was the driving force behind his evil intent to destroy David. And with an unrelenting jealous rage, Saul put everything else in his kingdom life on hold just so he could go after David. That is what the enemy does!

David describes his enemy. "My strong enemy ... those who hated me. For they were too strong for me. They confronted me in the day of my calamity" (Psalm 18:17–18).

David's enemy was very real. David had come face-to-face with his enemy, and the battle between them ensued. David had to run for his very life. And he kept on running. He had to do everything possible to escape from the evil king who sought after him. David spent time hiding out in caves, hoping not to be found by the king and his men. So many times, David faced that proverbial wall, hoping he would not go splat against it. David did what he knew he had to do in order to keep himself safe.

What David found in the midst of his battle with King Saul, greatly encourages me in the midst of my own battles of life. "But the Lord was my support" (Psalm 18:18b).

I love those words of David. I so often have echoed them from my own lips to the listening ears of God. "In my distress I called upon the Lord and cried out to my God; He heard my voice from the temple and my cry came before Him, even to His ears" (Psalm 18:6).

Ah, how good it is to know that we are never alone in the midst of our battles. We all can cry out to God from the battlefield. He will hear us. David cried out to God in the midst of his distress. And David found that God was there with him right in the midst of the battle. God was not sitting on the sidelines, cheering him on. God was present on the battlefield, right there with David, making known to him the way that he should go. God gave David all the resources he needed to face the enemy troops. God never once allowed David to go splat against the wall that was put up in front of, behind, and all around him. God enabled David to leap over that wall. God strengthened David for the battle of his life.

Here is what God did for David:

> He delivered me from my strong enemy. (Psalm 18:17)

> He also brought me out into a broad place; He delivered me because He delighted in me. (Psalm 18:19)

> The Lord rewarded me according to my righteousness. (Psalm 18:20)

> It is God who arms me with strength and make my way perfect. (Psalm 18:32)

> You have also given me the shield of Your salvation; Your right hand has held me up, Your gentleness has made me great. (Psalm 18:35)

> You enlarged my path under me, so my feet did not slip. (Psalm 18:36)

> You armed me with strength for the battle; You have subdued under me those who rose up against me. (Psalm 18:39)

> You have also given me the necks of my enemies, so that I destroyed those who hated me. (Psalm 18:40)

Wow! God did all that for David! Imagine what God can do for you and for me on the battlefield in the midst of our battles of life.

God promises to be with us. He will be present in the midst of our battles. He will be our support. He will give us strength. He will bring us to the place of victory. He will be our solid rock!

How do we get that kind of help from God? It starts with a cry. It starts with us acknowledging our need for God. We need His help. Cry out to Him. Call on His name. Invite Him to the battlefield. Let Him gird you with His strength. Take on His helmet of salvation, adorn the garments of praise in the midst of battle. Watch God fight for you, as He holds you tight with His mighty right hand. He will strike down each and every enemy. He will be the one who destroys them all. He will bring victory over all evil within and without. He will not cause your feet to slip or to stumble; rather, He will lift you up to high places, where you will stand strong. You will stand undefeated. The Lord, your God, will support you!

It is no wonder that in that moment after the battle was won, David wanted nothing more than to stand in the presence of his God and sing his victory song aloud.

"I will love You, O Lord, my strength. The Lord is my rock and my fortress and my deliverer; My God, my strength, in whom I will trust; My shield and the horn of my salvation, my stronghold. I will call upon the Lord, who is worthy to be praised, so shall I be saved from my enemies … The Lord lives! Blessed be my Rock! Let the God of my salvation be exalted" (Psalm 18:1–4, 46).

Oh, That I Had the Wings of a Dove!

Give ear to my prayer, O God, and do not hide
Yourself from my supplication. Attend to me
and hear me; I am restless in my complaint,
and moan noisily, because of the voice of
the enemy, because of the oppression of the
wicked; For they bring down trouble upon
me, and in wrath they hate me. My heart is
severely pained within me, and the terrors
of death have fallen upon me. Fearfulness
and trembling have come upon me. So, I said,
"Oh, that I had wings like a dove! I would fly
away and be at rest. Indeed, I would wander
far off, and remain in the wilderness."
—Psalm 55:1-7

Ever have one of those days when everything seems to go wrong, when nothing is going the right way, or when you find yourself wondering why you even got out of bed? You are troubled and distraught over circumstances beyond your control. You are overwhelmed and fearful of news that you just received from the doctor. You are not certain whether you will have a job tomorrow. You wonder where your children's next meal is going to come from. You hope you will be able to pay this month's rent in time. You simply want to run far, far, far away from the stresses and struggles of your life. Ever have one of those days?

Take heart! The psalmist David knows exactly how you feel. He was no stranger to the tough, discouraging, frustrating, overwhelming moments of life. He faced many a crisis. Psalm 55 records one of those days.

We do not know the specific details of the circumstances in this psalm, and we really do not need to know. But we do know that the problem involved one of David's closest companions, as he gives us that clue later in the chapter (Psalm 55:13): "But it is you, a man my equal, my companion, my close friend."

Obviously, David was betrayed by his close friend. Reading through these first seven verses of the psalm, we realize that David was deeply hurt. And that hurt led to the desire to run away. Ever have one of those days?

I am almost certain that every person reading this can relate to David's emotional cry when he says, "Oh, that I had wings like a dove! I would fly away and be at rest" (Psalm 55:6). David also said he would "wander far off ... [and] would hasten [his] escape" (Psalm 55:7).

Have you ever had one of those days?

If you could run away from your life's hardships and struggles right now, where would you go? Would you

- go back to bed and cover your head;
- head for the bathroom, lock yourself in, and have a good cry;
- call your mom or a close friend and meet for lunch and a good chat;
- head out for a spa day;
- go to the freezer, grab a container of ice cream, pick up a spoon, and savor every single bit until the container is empty;

- break out the credit card, get into the car, drive to the mall, and go shopping; or
- do something else?

David ran to the place that I would like to go to—that place I should go to every time I want to run away from life and its struggles. But it is the one place I do not run to as often as I should. David ran to God! Just read this: "As for me, I will call upon God, and the Lord shall save me. Evening and morning and at noon I will pray and cry aloud, and He shall hear my voice. He has redeemed my soul in peace from the battle that was against me" (Psalm 55:16–18).

Running to God is the safest thing to do! He loves! He listens! He cares! He will comfort! He will give advice! He will renew your strength! He will eat ice cream with you!

Oh, that we would hasten our escape to Him. He is waiting patiently for us. He is listening to our cries for help. We really do not have to be overwhelmed with life. We really do not have to struggle with the circumstances of our lives. Do not run away! We have just got to learn to fly! Fly to the God of David. You can do this. Spread your wings and fly to Him!

David gives us one final word of encouragement: "Cast your burden on the Lord, and He shall sustain you; He shall never permit the righteous to be moved" (Psalm 55:22). He will take that burden, no matter how big it is, away from you!

Oh, that we all could learn a life-changing lesson from the psalmist David. When you are having one of those days and simply want to run away from it all, consider following David's example instead. Mount your dove's wings and fly! Fly straight to the God who eagerly awaits you. Find your rest in the God who cares for you!

The Cry Must Come
Before the Calm

Then they cry to the Lord in their trouble,
and He brings them out of their distresses.
He calms the storm, so that its waves are
still. Then they are glad because they are
quiet; so, He guides them to their desired
haven. Oh, that men would give thanks
to the Lord for His goodness and for His
wonderful works to the children of men!
—Psalm 107:28–31

I am reasonably certain that everyone who is reading this right now is familiar with the storms of life. Cloudy skies, gusting winds, stormy waters, and pouring rain are all signs of storms within our atmosphere. Yet these same signs can be present in our daily lives as we experience storms in our homes, our relationships, our workplaces, our communities, and our own bodies. Storms can build up and roll in gradually, or they can come about quickly, almost unexpectedly. Storms can howl and hinder and create the worst kind of havoc. Storms can be utterly devastating, leaving paths of destruction in their wake that are hard to recover from. No one likes to go through stormy periods in their lives. Yet each one of us, at one point of time or another, will experience the storms of life.

The question is, What do we do in the midst of those storms? How do we cope with them? Is it possible to survive the worst of the storms and come out of it in one piece? What can we do to help weather the storms of life when they hit us? I would like to share ten things that we need to know about the storms of life—ten things that just might help us survive and come out of the storms only to find rest in a safe, calm haven.

1. Storms come to us all. Every one of us will face times when the seas rumble and roar around us, when our ships (our very beings) are tossed to and fro, when we fear for our very lives, and when we simply do not know what to do. We can expect storms as a part of our living.
2. Storms can (and often do) come at us unexpectedly. They have a way of catching us off guard. They can even throw us overboard if we are not careful.
3. When we are caught in a tempestuous storm of life and we are being tempest-tossed by the wind and waves, know that there is a master of that storm. Someone is in control of it. Our storm of life may be a storm that we brought on ourselves by something that we did. Our storm of life may be a tool that Satan is using to cause havoc, shipwreck, and even ruin. Our storm of life may be guided by God to bring us to a point of faith and trust in Him alone. And we have to know that if God is the Master of our storm, then this storm will not cease until the Master says, "Peace, be still!" (Mark 4:39).
4. During a storm of life, we can choose to aimlessly drift as the storm rages around us. But this choice comes with a serious warning: more damage to our

vessel is caused by aimlessly drifting, and shipwreck is almost certain. Prepare a plan of action in advance; consider what you will do when the storms come. Have a clear and definitive plan of action. Plan not to drift about aimlessly.

5. During the storm of life, we can choose not to despair. Yes, we may have to ride the storm out and endure whatever comes our way. But as we ride the wave, we need not despair. Seek God in the storm. If we set our eyes upon Him and watch for His deliverance, we will not despair. Hang on to the hope that He gives us for such a time. Hope in His presence, for He is with you in the storm. Hope in His purpose; every storm has a purpose, and in time, God will reveal that purpose to you. Hope in His promises; oh, so many of God's precious promises can be claimed during the storm. There is no need to despair when we have a solid hope that is found in our Savior.

6. During the storm, drop your anchor. For the Christian, this anchor is the very Word of God! Wrap your heart around that anchor; drop it into the storm. It will help you remain steady, strong, and stable. As the winds and waves whip around you, God's Word is the anchor that enables you to focus not so much upon the storm as on the Master of the storm. Get into God's Word; read it, meditate upon it, obey it, wrap your heart and soul around it. Let God's Word be the anchor that it is to you.

7. During the storm, do not forget about nourishment. We need the spiritual nourishment of God's Word in our hearts and lives during any storm. But we also need to be reminded, at times, to seek physical nourishment. Eat well. Eat often. Eat even when you do not feel like eating. Eat and nourish your body, heart, and soul.

8. Wait out the storm. No matter how long it lasts, wait it out. No matter how battered you feel, wait it out. No matter whether you feel all hope is gone, wait it out. If God is present, hope is still there! No matter whether you crash, wait it out. God has a purpose for each storm of life you endure; wait it out. He wants you to learn valuable lessons; wait it out. He wants to be your Savior in that storm; wait it out. He wants to hear your cries for help and as you pray to Him; wait it out. He wants to show you what He can do; wait it out.

9. At the end of the storm, praise the God of the storm. Praise Him all the more when He speaks peace into your storm. It is by grace and grace alone that we have come through the storms of life. We will survive to tell the story of the storms.

10. Do not be afraid to share your personal story of storms you have endured, for in the sharing, you may be the instrument God uses to help save another in their storm. Your story will inspire those who hear it. Your story can be used to save a life. Your story will bring praise, honor, and glory to your God.

Storms of life happen to all of us. When the storms of life come, know that you are never alone in the midst of them. God will be ever present with you in the storm. He keeps His promise to "never leave you nor forsake you" (Hebrews 13:5). Never be afraid to call out to God during your next storm. He will be listening for your cry, and He will answer you. In Him and His Word, through His grace, you will find an anchor for your soul that will carry you safely through the storm.

But remember, the cry must come before the calm! Trust your next storm to the One, who hears your cry and brings the calm after the storm. He will carry you through the storm to a safe, calm haven!

What Motivates You to Pray?

O God, You are my God; early will I seek
You; my soul thirsts for You; my flesh longs
for You ... So, I have looked for You.
—Psalm 63:1

What motivates you to pray? What is your motive for starting a prayer life? What motivates you to have a conversation from time to time with your God?

Here's how a couple of my friends responded when I asked them those questions:

"A prayer life, for me, was a process of going through the motions. I was a Christian, went to church every week. I did what was expected of me. But then I stopped praying."

"As the years have drifted by, for me it was all about the mechanics of prayer and Bible study and going to church. My motivations were all wrong, of course. But if I am completely honest, I have to admit that very little seemed to sink into even my brain, let alone my heart. I was being spoon-fed my spiritual food, and I did not like to process things for myself. I was too caught up in playing the part of a Christian to be concerned about the depth of my spiritual life. Occasionally a crisis would pop up in my life, and then I would pray. I prayed as hard as I could until the crisis was over. God was not one bit fooled by my emergency prayers.

I could almost hear Him say to me, 'How come you never talk to me unless you are in some kind of crisis?' That was a very valid point, especially considering the fact that I basically ignored Him for most of the time."

"I became motivated to pray when I lost my job and my family almost lost our home. I felt like I was forced to pray to God and ask Him for His help. At least I understood that there was a God who could help me, and I turned to Him for help."

"Motivation in prayer came to me when I was at camp. The speaker was pretty forceful about 'developing a prayer life with God.' So I guess more out of fear than anything else, I started praying that week of camp. By the end of the week, I started enjoying my chats with God and wanted to keep having them every day. I did okay for a while but then started slacking off again."

"My motivation comes from my relationship with Him. He loves me, and I know that so well. But I want to love Him too. And I just figure that we have to talk, to share, to spend time together if that love relationship between me and God will ever grow."

What is your motivation to pray?

I think that, as Christians, each of our answers could be similar to or different from the next person's. I think that while we each might have a relationship with God, each relationship is different and in a different place from the next person's. In other words, I do not think there is a right or wrong answer to those questions. Yet I do believe that they are good questions to think about.

I have to tell you that a teenage student of mine asked me that question—"What is your motivation to pray?" And yes, I needed some time to reflect and consider my honest answer to that question. I made a list of various answers I could give to my student. All of them were true at various points of my life and within different circumstances that

I was going through during those points. Here are some of the things that I listed:

- ✓ a need for God's help
- ✓ a friend who asked me to pray for them
- ✓ an emergency situation
- ✓ a big decision that I needed to make and did not know what to do
- ✓ a challenge from the pastor at church to pray more
- ✓ a specific prayer request
- ✓ a heavy financial need
- ✓ so many more self-motivated points

But at the end of my thinking about it, I simply had to change the question. Yes, you read that correctly. I wanted to change my student's question. I needed to change it for my own thinking. But I also wanted to challenge my student to think deeper into his own question. Perhaps we all should change that question. So consider this.

I began to ask God, "God, what do *You* want my motivation to be in prayer?" I waited for His answer.

It came just a few days later, in my Bible reading for the day, at the very first verse of Psalm 63. One verse—that was all I read that day. That one verse gripped my heart like none other had for quite a while. One verse stuck in my memory for over a week as God ministered the meaning of that one verse to my heart and soul. One verse answered my question and changed my viewpoint as to what motivates me to pray. Here is that one verse: "Oh God, You are my God; early will I seek You; my soul thirsts for You, my flesh longs for You ... So, I have looked for You" (Psalm 63:1).

God should be my motivation to pray! A desire to grow my relationship with my God should be the only motivation I need to pray, for "You are my God!" (Psalm 63:1).

My thirsty soul should be my motivation to pray!

The longing of my heart, body, and flesh should be my motivation to pray!

God should be all the motivation I need to pray, to talk to, to converse with, to commune with, to bond with, or to unite with God.

So I will look for Him! I will seek after Him! I will begin a conversation with Him! Through the avenue of prayer, I will be motivated to grow my personal relationship with Him!

O God, You are my God! I love praying to You!

Make Haste, O God

Make haste, O God, to deliver me! Make haste
to help me, O Lord! Let them be ashamed and
confounded who seek my life; let them be
turned back and confused who desire my hurt.
Let them be turned back because of their
shame, who say, 'Aha! Aha!' Let all those who
seek You rejoice and be glad in You; and let
those who love Your salvation say continually,
'Let God be magnified!' But I am poor and
needy; make haste to me, O God! You are my
help and my deliverer; O Lord, do not delay.
—Psalm 70:1-5

Make haste! Hurry! Be quick! Do not delay!

Sadly, we live in a society nowadays that likes to have things done in a hurry. We do not want to wait. We do not like to wait!

Here are some of the people, on any given day, that we might say "Hurry!" to:

- our kids, while trying to get them out the door and off to school
- our spouses, as they are taking their time getting ready for a dinner date

- a person we just interviewed with, as we wait for their answer regarding a job we would like to have
- the cashier at the grocery store checking someone out ahead of us at a very slow pace
- the barista serving up our cup of coffee while we are on our run to work
- a doctor as we await a phone call regarding our test results
- the mailman delivering a check to us
- a boss who is to give us a long-awaited promotion
- our boyfriends or girlfriends as we await the magical "Will you marry me?"

We are a people who are in a constant hurry. We want everyone around us to make haste!

What about saying, "Hurry!" to God? Have you ever in your prayers, while presenting a request to Him, implied or stated directly that you would like God to hurry with the answer? "Please God, don't delay. Be quick. Are you listening to me? I need that answer today!"

This reminds me of the psalmist David and what he said in Psalm 70. This is undoubtedly one of many psalms written when David was being harassed by King Saul. King Saul was jealous of David and sought after his very life. David obviously made a quick request of God to help him, perhaps to rescue him from this one who wanted to kill him. And David, in that moment, would have loved a quick answer back from God. "Make haste, O God!" David says not once, not twice, but three times. "Make haste to help me, O Lord!" (Psalm 70:1).

What was up with the urgency? David says, "I am poor and needy" (Psalm 70:5). Whatever David was facing in this exact moment, he realized more than anything that he needed God's help. He could not face whatever it was alone. He knew that King Saul was after him; he knew that evil surrounded him. And he knew that God would be his helper and deliverer. And so he prayed. He cried out for God to "Make haste!"

It is a really good thing to call upon God for help and deliverance. We can all cry out to Him in all kinds of situations. There is no situation, no set of circumstances, no battle, no concern, and no worry that is too big for God to help us with and to deliver us from. Yet, with us being a people that always seem to be in a hurry, waiting for God's answer is usually not something that we want to do or something that we like to do.

Have you ever pondered the delays of God? Oftentimes it does seem that God is delaying His answers to us. We wait, and He seems silent. We wonder if He even heard our prayer. We question the delay. We might even get mad at God because He does not "make haste" and hurry to help us. When was the last time you experienced one of those delays from God?

I have to tell you something that you might not want to hear. God is never in a hurry! Never! He will never work on our "make haste, hurry, don't delay" time schedule. He will always work on His own schedule in His perfect timing and according to His holy will. And, truth be told, that is a really hard lesson for those of us who are always rushing, always in a hurry, and always waiting for that answer to arrive *now*.

God is never in a hurry, but once He starts working, watch out! His work is amazing! He patiently accomplishes His perfect work, oftentimes behind the scenes where we don't see it. But when we do not see it, we automatically think He is not there, is not listening, and is not working. We could, just maybe, be wrong about God in that regard.

If, right now, it seems to you that God is

- silent instead of listening,
- resting instead of moving,

- tarrying instead of working,
- delaying instead of acting, or
- helping others instead of you,

then know that there are some things that you can do. You cannot make God move any faster than He wants to. You do not have the ability to hurry Him up in the process of answering. But after you have cried out for His help, and while you wait for His answer, there are a few things that you can do.

1. You can *seek* Him. Look at the first part of verse 4 in Psalm 70. It says, "Let all those who seek You rejoice and be glad in You." Seek Him in the reading of His Word. Seek Him as you learn more about who God is. Seek Him as you continue to pray to God. Seek Him as you search for His will in the answer to your prayer request. Seek His help as you wait for the answer. Seek after His joy and gladness. Just seek Him!

2. You can *wait* for Him. Present your request, your need, and your concerns to God. And then wait. Wait for His timetable to accomplish an answer. Wait for Him to do whatever work behind the scenes He needs to do to bring about your answer. Wait, and do not give up. Yield not to the temptation to take matters into your own hands and create a complete disaster because you could not wait. Wait with patience. Even when waiting is hard, wait with patience. In the end, you will be glad that you waited for His perfect answer.

3. You can *love* Him. Look at the last part of verse 4. It says, "... and let those who love Your salvation say continually, 'Let God be magnified.'" Please, do not get angry at God because you think He is not

there for you, not listening to you, or not willing to help you. That is the farthest thing from the truth. God is there! Right now, God is there for you! He dearly loves you and wants to help you. He wants you to accept His love that He has for you. Perhaps, in the midst of waiting for Him to answer your cry for help, it's a good time to reflect on His love for you. Oh, dear reader, might I encourage you to make haste and seek God, wait for Him, and love Him. You might just be glad that you did. You might just rejoice in His answer. You might just say out loud when the answer to your prayer is delivered, "Let God be magnified!" (Psalm 70:4).

I encourage you to try it and see what happens.

Hurry now. Do not delay. God is listening for your voice! He will hear it!

Rain Showers of Scripture

Oh, love the Lord, all you, His saints! For
the Lord preserves the faithful, ... Be of
good courage, and He shall strengthen
your heart, all you who hope in the Lord.
—Psalm 31:23-24

It was the very wee hours of the morning. It was dark outside and dark in the house. A little night-light shone dimly in the hallway. I tossed and turned as I tried to get a little more comfortable in my warm bed. It was time to face the facts. I simply could not sleep.

So I quietly got up, not wanting to disturb anyone else in the house. I made my way to the kitchen, filled the kettle with some water, and fixed myself a nice cup of hot tea. Once that was done, I curled up in my favorite chair in the living room. The dog nestled down on my lap for a chance of another nap. I picked up my Bible from the table beside me. And I settled down for a good read before the early morning hours got interrupted with noise and chaos.

Psalm 31 was the place my bookmark indicated for my reading on this particular morning. It is a psalm of trust. Trust and hope seemed to have been my key words of thought over the past week as I encountered many a trial and difficult circumstance of life. I trust God wholeheartedly. My hope is in Him alone. Yet, as I have already learned in life, my hope and trust can be tested at times. And lately it seemed they were being tested a lot more than usual. I know, through experience, that hope and trust can be, and often do need to be, renewed. I know that I need a gentle reminder from time to time to trust in God and place my hope with Him.

On this cold winter's morning, as I sat curled up in my chair, all warm and cozy, I could hear a gentle rain coming down outside, surrounding our house and garden with some much-needed moisture that only the darkness knew at this point. Soon daylight would come. And yet my heart had hopes that it would just keep on raining. I longed for a cold, cloudy, and rainy day—a day on which I could stay curled up and be warm within the walls of my home.

As I sat and read and meditated and prayed over God's Word, I was refreshed. It felt like a rain shower to my soul—a gentle rain sent by God to wash away my concerns, at least for a little space of time. The wonderful words of scripture brought me peace. It reminded me of God's faithfulness to me. I soaked in those words as though they were moisture from the cool rain, allowing them to refresh the parched, dry ground of my heart.

As you read through these words of Psalm 31, let them fall like fresh rain upon your soul. Soak in their refreshment. Let them wash away your concerns. Let them renew your trust and bring you hope for the day.

> In You, O Lord, I put my trust. (Psalm 31:1)
> Be my rock of refuge, a fortress of defense to save me. (Psalm 31:2)
> For You are my rock and my fortress; therefore, for Your names' sake, lead and guide me. (Psalm 31:3)
> For You are my strength. (Psalm 31:4)
> Into Your hand I commit my spirit; You have redeemed me, O Lord God of truth. (Psalm 31:5)

I will be glad and rejoice in Your mercy, for You have considered my trouble; You have known my soul in adversities. (Psalm 31:7)

But as for me, I trust in You, O Lord; I say, "You are my God." (Psalm 31:14)

My times are in Your hand. (Psalm 31:15)

Make Your face to shine upon Your servant; save me for Your mercies' sake. (Psalm 31:16)

Do not let me be ashamed, O Lord, for I have called upon You. (Psalm 31:17)

Oh, how great is Your goodness, which You have laid up for those who fear You, which You have prepared for those who trust in You. (Psalm 31:19)

Blessed be the Lord, for He has shown me His marvelous kindness. (Psalm 31:21)

You heard the voice of my supplications when I cried out to You. (Psalm 31:22)

Oh, love the Lord, all you, His saints! For the Lord preserves the faithful. (Psalm 31:23)

Be of good courage, and He shall strengthen your heart, all you who hope in the Lord. (Psalm 31:24)

Just let those scripture verses rain down upon your heart and soul. Read through them again if you need to.

Take a moment and just stand in awe of your God! Give thought to who He is. Consider what He has done for you. His great love is faithful and true. That love grows stronger each day. His love washes over your soul. His kindness and mercy bring refreshment to your heart. It is just like the rain shower outside that brings refreshment to the dry ground, only this rain shower brings His refreshment to your heart and soul. Just let it rain!

Stand in the rain shower of scripture! Refresh and renew your trust, your hope, and your love in the Lord your God. Stand in total awe of who He is, for He is your God!

I Will Extol You, My God

I will extol You, my God, O King; and I will bless
Your name forever and ever. Every day I will
bless You, and I will praise Your name forever
and ever. Great is the Lord, and greatly to be
praised; and His greatness is unsearchable.
One generation shall praise Your works to
another and shall declare Your mighty acts.
I will meditate on the glorious splendor of
Your majesty, and on Your wondrous works.
Men shall speak of the might of Your awesome
acts, and I will declare Your greatness.
They shall utter the memory of Your great
goodness and shall sing of Your righteousness.
—Psalm 145:1-7

My day was over! My body, heart, and soul were exhausted!
I had done my best to keep a positive attitude throughout
the day, but lately I find it hard to do most days. The news
of the day is filled with the coronavirus pandemic and the
social distancing we must do from one another. Sports
activities, restaurants, churches, libraries, and so much
more have all been shut down. The amount of traffic on the
streets is becoming a little less. Appointments and meetings
are getting cancelled. Grocery stores have become zoos as
shelves are emptied and people fight to get the last of that

day's supplies. Our doctors, nurses, and essential workers are exhausted from long hours of working among the sick and dying from this virus that is spreading so rapidly. Many people are quarantined in their homes, trying to work and teach school to their children. This has been called our new normal, but I call it crazy. I never thought I would see anything like this in my lifetime!

My husband and I are currently working through a period of surgical recovery, with limited income and uncertain days ahead. Major decisions have to be made that are exhausting to think about, and it is difficult to imagine what the future might hold for us. There are all the usual things that still need to be done: beds to be made, people and a dog to feed, food to cook, laundry to get done, rooms to dust, floors to mop, weeds in the yard to pull, and house repairs to consider. There are people we would love to see, but we cannot see them because of the need for social distancing, and thus the battle of cabin fever and isolation is ongoing. There are new limitations and precautions to observe in order to be safe. Our life, as we once knew it, has changed! And some days (most days, if I am really honest) it is all so very exhausting!

But now my day is done. I slipped out on the back porch, sat down on a patio chair, and let out a tired sigh. It was this kind of quiet I had longed for all day.

As I sat there, I looked up into the sky. *Beautiful!* I enjoyed the sights of the stars and the moon shining through a few clouds that still lingered in the night sky. I could hear the owl hooting from up in the forty-foot pine tree that graces the yard. Somehow, all this brought peace to my heart. Right now, I welcome peace!

And then, within that peaceful moment, my thoughts turned toward God. I thought about the crazy day and rejoiced in the thought that God is the one who is in total control of all the chaos right now. It really is not the world leaders, politicians, scientists, or medical personnel who have control of this pandemic right now, as some would have us believe. There's one more powerful who oversees it all.

I trust God's control more than that of any human being. His plan is perfect for me, for my life, for my marriage, for my home, for my ministry, for my community, and for this world that I live in. It is all under His perfect and timely control. Just the thought of God's perfect plan brings me great peace!

As I sat there reflecting on God and enjoying the beautiful night sky, the words to a Bible verse popped into my mind: "Great is the Lord and greatly to be praised." I once learned a little chorus with those words. I sang them softly as I sat on the back porch, gazing into the night sky.

After a restful little while, I went back into the house. I wanted my Bible. Now, where had I put it? The search was on. I had to find the reference to that Bible verse that came to my mind out on the back porch. I do not like to admit this, but my mind has a hard time remembering Bible references these days. I was just so happy that I knew the verse. Anyway, I searched, and soon, I found what I was looking for: Psalm 145:3.

But then something else really stood out to me as I read the entire chapter of Psalm 145. I knew I had read this psalm many times before, but on this particular night, these verses just jumped off the page at me. It seemed as though God was telling me something.

I noticed five "I will" statements written by the psalmist David. Psalm 145 is a song written by David as a song of praise. It is not a song of praise to himself or about himself. Nor is it written to someone else in his life. No, this is a song of praise that is directed to his gracious God. And in that psalm, he states five things that he will do. On this particular night, those five things inspired me. Allow me to share those five things with you.

1. "I will extol You" (Psalm 145:1). I believe the word "extol" means "to praise something or someone in the highest of terms," or "to simply magnify someone or something." David's heart's desire was to praise and to magnify his God. David says that this praise was for "My God, O King." With this "I will," David gives praise to his God, the King of his life. David magnifies his God, his King. And as I read the remainder of that psalm, I realized that David had plenty to say about his God. Hmm, do I do that?

2. "I will bless Your name" (Psalm 145:2). To me the word "bless" means "to invoke or to place a divine favor upon a person or thing; to glorify someone; to make someone happy, as by giving someone a gift." David said, "I will bless Your name forever and ever. Every day I will bless You." Did you catch that? Every day! Forever and ever! David purposed in his heart and expressed it in the song of praise to his gracious God that he would bless Him. He did not say, "I will bless You only when I feel like it" or "I will bless You on days I remember to." No! David's heart's desire was to get into the habit of blessing the Lord, his God, every day. Hmm, do I do that?

3. "I will praise Your name" (Psalm 145:3). To me the word "praise" means "to express approval of someone or something, as by giving applause or expressing words of adoration." It also means "to commend one's good work, giving notice to a job well done." Praise was important to David. Again his heart's desire was to praise God often. He says, "Great is the Lord, and greatly to be praised; and His greatness is unsearchable" (Psalm 145:3). David recognized the greatness of God and the greatness of His handiwork in the things God created. David saw the greatness of His love that God poured out often upon David,

91

and the greatness of His deeds in the things that He did for David. David acknowledged and praised his great God, stating that He is greatly to be praised. God deserves the praises of His people.

David goes even further to say, "One generation shall praise Your works to another and shall declare Your mighty acts" (Psalm 145:4). David wanted to teach the next generation how to praise God as well. Thus he wrote so many of the songs that we find in Israel's songbook of praise. Even in our generations of today, we are still inspired to praise our God through the songs we sing, the words we speak, and the thoughts we consider. Hmm, do I do that?

4. "I will meditate" (Psalm 145:5). I like the word "meditate," for to me it means "to really think about something; to consider something deeply within the thought processes." Meditation is good for the soul. Everyone needs time to quietly think about things. David knew he needed that time too. He chose to meditate upon his God. Just what, about God, did he meditate upon? He tells us. "I will meditate on the glorious splendor of Your majesty, and on Your wondrous works" (Psalm 145:5). Hmm, do I do that?

5. "I will declare Your greatness" (Psalm 145:6). To me the word "declare" means "to simply state something positively or emphatically." David wanted to tell abroad the greatness of his God. He did not care what other people thought. He boldly announced to the world what he thought of his God. Hmm, do I do that?

David said rather boldly, "I will extol; I will bless; I will praise; I will meditate; I will declare."

Those five things jumped out at me as I sat reading this psalm. I know in my head and in my heart that this is a really good thing to do all the time, and especially during times of crisis, of uncertainty, and of chaos.

But I had to pause and ask myself these questions: Do I do that? Do I extol my God in any way? Do I bless Him for the work He does in my life? Do I praise Him just because He is worthy of my praise? Do I meditate on Him, on His Word, often enough? Do I declare His greatness to those around me?

Do you want to know my answer?

In all honesty, I have to answer that yes, I do! I do all five of those things. I just do not do them nearly as often as I should. I could do a whole lot better at extolling, at blessing, at praising, at meditating, and at declaring my God. Why? Because I agree with the psalmist David. His God—my God, our God—is "great and greatly to be praised" (Psalm 145:3).

David boldly and unashamedly announces to many generations, through his writing of Psalm 145, what he thinks about His great God and King, the Lord of his life. It is his song of praise.

> The Lord is gracious and full of compassion, slow to anger and great in mercy. The Lord is good to all, and His tender mercies are over all His works. All Your works shall praise You, O Lord, and Your saints shall bless You. They shall speak of the glory of Your kingdom, and talk of Your power, to make known to the sons of men His mighty acts and the glorious majesty of His kingdom. Your kingdom is an everlasting kingdom, and Your dominion endures throughout all generations. The Lord upholds all who fall and raises up all who are bowed down. The eyes of all look expectantly to You, and You give them their food in due season. You open Your hand and satisfy the desire of every living thing. The Lord is righteous in all His

ways, gracious in all His works. The Lord is near to all who call upon Him, to all who call upon Him in truth. He will fulfill the desire of those who fear Him; He also will hear their cry and save them. The Lord preserves all who love Him, but all the wicked He will destroy. My mouth shall speak the praise of the Lord, and all flesh shall bless His holy name forever and ever. (Psalm 145:8–21)

I do not know about you, but I just love the way David praises his God. The sheer honesty of his heart before his God is inspiring! I could truly learn a lesson or two from him. David has encouraged me to spend more time praising God, during these crazy days of life on this earth with the God that I love.

I will extol, bless, praise, meditate upon, and declare the greatness of my God! I will do that a little louder, a little longer, a little more boldly and a little more unashamedly! I will stand with the psalmist David and proudly declare, "Great is the Lord and greatly to be praised!"

About the Author

Kathy O'Brien, a missionary teacher for thirty-eight years, has served in Edinburgh, Scotland, and Liverpool, England, and now in Tucson, Arizona. Kathy is also the director of Word of Truth Ministries, a children's Bible correspondence and discipleship ministry that reaches out to children ages five to eighteen, teaching them of God's love and encouraging them to grow in relationship with God. She and husband, Andrew, live in Tucson.

Visit her online at www.word-of-truth-ministries.com.

Printed in the United States
by Baker & Taylor Publisher Services